AWAKEN
YOUR INDIGO
POWER

Angels 101
Angel Guidance Board
Crystal Therapy (with Judith Lukomski)
Connecting with Your Angels Kit (includes booklet, CD, journal, etc.)
The Crystal Children
Archangels & Ascended Masters
Earth Angels
Messages from Your Angels
Angel Visions II
Eating in the Light (with Becky Black, M.F.T., R.D.)
The Care and Feeding of Indigo Children
Angel Visions
Divine Prescriptions
Healing with the Angels
"I'd Change My Life If I Had More Time"
Divine Guidance
Chakra Clearing
Angel Therapy®
Constant Craving A–Z
Constant Craving
The Yo-Yo Diet Syndrome
Losing Your Pounds of Pain

Audio/CD Programs

Don't Let Anything Dull Your Sparkle (unabridged audio book)
The Healing Miracles of Archangel Raphael (unabridged audio book)
Angel Therapy® Meditations
Archangels 101 (abridged audio book)
Solomon's Angels (unabridged audio book)
Fairies 101 (abridged audio book)
Angel Medicine
Angels Among Us (with Michael Toms)
Messages from Your Angels (abridged audio book)
Past-Life Regression with the Angels
Divine Prescriptions
The Romance Angels
Connecting with Your Angels
Manifesting with the Angels
Karma Releasing
Healing Your Appetite, Healing Your Life
Healing with the Angels
Divine Guidance
Chakra Clearing

DVD Program

How to Give an Angel Card Reading

Calendar

Angel Affirmations (for each individual year)

Card Decks

Butterfly Oracle Cards for Life Changes
Loving Words from Jesus
Fairy Tarot Cards (with Radleigh Valentine)
Archangel Gabriel Oracle Cards
Angel Answers Oracle Cards (with Radleigh Valentine)
Past Life Oracle Cards (with Brian Weiss, M.D.)
Guardian Angel Tarot Cards (with Radleigh Valentine)
Cherub Angel Cards for Children
Talking to Heaven Mediumship Cards (with James Van Praagh)
Archangel Power Tarot Cards (with Radleigh Valentine)
Flower Therapy Oracle Cards (with Robert Reeves, N.D.)
Angel Dreams Oracle Cards (with Melissa Virtue)
Mary, Queen of Angels Oracle Cards
Angel Tarot™ Cards (with Radleigh Valentine and Steve A. Roberts)
The Romance Angels Oracle Cards
Life Purpose Oracle Cards
Archangel Raphael Healing Oracle Cards
Archangel Michael Oracle Cards
Angel Therapy® Oracle Cards
Magical Messages from the Fairies Oracle Cards
Ascended Masters Oracle Cards
Daily Guidance from Your Angels Oracle Cards
Saints & Angels Oracle Cards
Magical Unicorns Oracle Cards
Goddess Guidance Oracle Cards
Archangel Oracle Cards
Magical Mermaids and Dolphins Oracle Cards
Messages from Your Angels Oracle Cards
Healing with the Fairies Oracle Cards
Healing with the Angels Oracle Cards

ALSO BY CHARLES VIRTUE

Book

Manifesting with the Angels

All of the above are available at your local bookstore,
or may be ordered through Hay House USA: www.hayhouse.com®; Hay House
Australia: www.hayhouse.com.au; Hay House UK: www.hayhouse.co.uk; Hay House
South Africa: www.hayhouse.co.za; Hay House India: www.hayhouse.co.in

Doreen's website: www.AngelTherapy.com

Charles's website: www.CharlesVirtue.com

AWAKEN
YOUR INDIGO
POWER

Harness Your Passion,
Fulfill Your Purpose, and Activate
Your Innate Spiritual Gifts

DOREEN VIRTUE
and CHARLES VIRTUE

HAY HOUSE, INC.
Carlsbad, California • New York City
London • Sydney • Johannesburg
Vancouver • New Delhi

Published and distributed in the United States by: Hay House, Inc.: www.hayhouse.com® • *Published and distributed in Australia by:* Hay House Australia Pty. Ltd.: www.hayhouse.com.au • *Published and distributed in the United Kingdom by:* Hay House UK, Ltd.: www.hay house.co.uk • *Published and distributed in the Republic of South Africa by:* Hay House SA (Pty), Ltd.: www.hayhouse.co.za • *Distributed in Canada by:* Raincoast Books: www.raincoast.com • *Published in India by:* Hay House Publishers India: www.hayhouse.co.in

Cover design: Tricia Breidenthal • *Interior design:* Pamela Homan

Library of Congress Cataloging-in-Publication Data

Names: Virtue, Doreen, date, author.
Title: Awaken your indigo power : harness your passion, fulfill your purpose,   and activate your innate spiritual gifts / Doreen Virtue and Charles   Virtue.
Description: Carlsbad : Hay House, Inc., 2016.
Identifiers: LCCN 2016037599 | ISBN 9781401943868 (tradepaper : alk. paper)
Subjects: LCSH: Self-realization--Miscellanea. | Self-actualization
   (Psychology)--Miscellanea. | Parapsychology. | Spirituality. | Indigo
   children.
Classification: LCC BF1999 .V58624 2016 | DDC 131--dc23 LC record available at https://lccn.loc.gov/2016037599

ISBN: 978-1-4019-4386-8

10 9 8 7 6 5 4 3 2 1
1st edition, November 2016

Printed in the United States of America

In order for change to come,
awareness must be present.
In order for awareness to exist,
one's eyes must be open,
and the best way to
open someone's eyes
is to show them the truth.

CONTENTS

PREFACE

by Doreen

When I was invited by author Lee Carroll to contribute chapters to his book *The Indigo Children* back in 1998,
it opened up a whole new world for me. As the mother of
two sons, Grant and Charles (who is the co-author of this
book), I always knew there was something special about
them. I'd also been a therapist at an adolescent outpatient
facility and was impressed by the intuitive intelligence of
the youth at my clinic.

I wondered if there were personality differences
between this generation of teenagers I was counseling
and the generation *I* had been born into. Researching and
writing about the Indigo generation answered questions
about my sons, my adolescent counseling clients, and
even myself and the world! (I'll share more details of these
discoveries in this book.)

When I wrote *The Care and Feeding of Indigo Children*
(Hay House, 2001), the Indigo generation was still largely
children, teenagers, and young adults. The book wasn't
written so much for the Indigos themselves as it was for
their parents, teachers, and guardians.

Charles helped me research *The Care and Feeding of
Indigo Children* by interviewing other youths and com-
piling data and extracting patterns. (He has since taught
about Indigos during his worldwide workshop tours, in
magazine and radio interviews, and in blogs and podcasts.)

The research opened Charles's eyes, too. We both realized that the "problems" he seemed to be experiencing at

school and home represented the double edge of a sword. On the one hand, Charles didn't automatically respect someone just because they held a title like "school principal." You had to *earn* Charles's respect and trust. On the other hand, he had the uncanny ability to sniff out dishonesty the moment he met anyone.

The interviews that Charles and I held with Indigos, their parents, and their teachers taught us that the Indigo generation had an inner truth detector. In a way, all sentient beings have this sense of knowing and feeling the energy of another person. The big difference, though, is that the Indigo generation never *doubts* their truth detector. Other generations are initially aware of internal warnings that they're with an untrustworthy person. But they soon talk themselves out of those feelings—and then are upset that they wind up in one more hurtful relationship.

They feel betrayed . . . but are they? Isn't it really a form of *self*-betrayal to ignore the warnings you're receiving from your gut feelings?

In the year 2000, while writing the book about Indigos, I had a realization that my Indigo son had been trying to teach me to trust my intuition all along. How many times had Charles warned me about a new "friend" or a business acquaintance, and then his warning proved to be merited?

The older generations are intuitive, too. I mean, I deliver Divine messages from guardian angels and archangels. And I'm really good at getting messages for other people. But for myself, in the past I'd sometimes struggle with trusting my intuition . . . until my son Charles taught me how to awaken my own Indigo Power!

Here's a fictional example to illustrate this concept:

A woman is shopping at the grocery store with her young Indigo son when a man approaches them. Both mother and son are startled by the man's loud voice and fast movements. Both of them have internal warning alarms going off.

The man makes nervous small talk, and it's obvious he wants something. There's the hidden-agenda vibe oozing from his mannerisms.

The Indigo son tugs at his mother's hand to leave the situation and says bluntly to the man, "We aren't interested." The woman blushes with embarrassment, believing her son is being rude. After all, she thinks, we shouldn't judge anyone. She mutters an excuse to the man to explain her son's behavior as she backs away to join him in the next aisle.

Indigos have a "Spidey sense" (like the Spider-Man superhero), and their whole body reacts to dishonesty. This is one reason why Indigos appear to be hyperactive and are often mislabeled as having attention deficit/hyperactivity disorder (ADHD). Their attention isn't deficient; it's just dialed in to the truth instead of the surface.

An Indigo can instantly detect a con artist, while older generations are ready to give that person a chance. The energy is physically painful to the Indigo, and they try to escape the cause (the dishonest person).

If they can't escape, as in a classroom setting with mandatory attendance, they will wiggle in their seats to discharge the energy. This is when they appear uninterested in school and hyperactive. These amazingly gifted Indigos are prescribed Ritalin and other psychoactive medications while the real problem goes unaddressed.

So, let's look at realistic ways for Indigos to receive an education without being traumatized or mislabeled. Let's examine the remarkable intuitive qualities of Indigos so that we *all* can benefit from the gifts this generation brings to the world.

INTRODUCTION

The Truth about Indigos

by Doreen and Charles

Whether you consider yourself an Indigo or not, this generation of truth-telling, confident leaders has much to teach us all. Imagine having 100 percent faith in your intuition and feeling a clear, passionate calling to your life purpose. These are among the gifts of the Indigo Power within you and everyone . . . as modeled by the positive example of the Indigos.

The purpose of the Indigo energy is to bring integrity back to the planet. No more "spinning" the truth by media, corporations, government, and other institutions. No more exploiting other people, animals, or the environment in order for companies to grow richer. That all stops now, because the Indigos are here.

The term *Indigo* may have negative connotations, associated with hyperactivity and defiance. Yes, it's true that Indigos are strong willed, and their unwillingness to compromise their values may have caused disruptions in their home and school life. Indigos are angry and passionate, and the fire in their eyes and edginess in their speech, body language, and fashion choices are unmistakable. They wear their anger on their sleeves, without apology. Indigos don't care what you think about them, and they are at peace with who they are.

But it's also true that many Indigos are fulfilling their destiny and changing the world in positive ways. Because they don't care about others' opinions, Indigos aren't swayed from their inner visions. They are now the innovators, inventors, and activists who are leading us away from corporate greed and into global caretaking.

The majority of Indigos were born in the 1970s, and they are now adults. However, there have always been Indigos on this planet, and we'll discuss some of the famous and world-changing examples in this book. Indigos are still being born, just not as frequently.

The main characteristics of the Indigo spirit and generation are:

- Strong will
- Blunt truthfulness, no matter what the consequences
- Idealism
- Fiery passion in their eyes
- Frustration and anger about world events
- Hypervigilance and constant alertness to perceived threats or danger
- Wariness until you prove your trustworthiness to them
- Unwillingness to compromise or sell out their values
- Trust in their intuition
- High standards
- Adherence to their own internal core convictions

- Edginess in their speech, mannerisms, hairstyle, body art, and clothing style

- Independence (often loners)

- Impulsivity

- Original thinking

Indigos are also . . .

- Comfortable with the shadows of life

- Intuitive and in touch with gut feelings

- Prone to mood swings

- Highly sensitive to chemicals

- Spiritual, not religious

In addition, Indigos . . .

- Follow their hearts

- Know the value of having fun

- Respect people only for what they do, not on account of age, wealth, or title

- Enjoy music

If you relate to the majority (not necessarily all) of these characteristics, this is a sign that you are an Indigo. Or if you're thinking of someone else, it indicates that the other person likely is one.

Indigo isn't a box category that you can neatly fit people into. It's actually a description of a personality and energy style with some very admirable traits that could serve us all. Our vision is a world where Indigo Power is unleashed at its highest vibrational potential.

There's a crossover of the term *Generation X* (referring to those born in the 1960s through 1970s) and Indigos, which we'll look at in this book. However, the notion that all Indigos were born in certain years is a fallacy—it's just that the majority were born in the 1970s.

We can envision a world where Indigo energy teaches us all to trust our gut feelings and to demand honesty and integrity from everyone. We see a world where it's no longer possible to be lied to or manipulated, because everyone can plainly see the truth . . . and speaks up about it. These are among the blessings that the Indigo generation has come to model for us all.

Doreen: As the mother of an Indigo, and as a former psychotherapist and director of an adolescent drug-and-alcohol outpatient treatment center, I am excited to share what I've learned as a parent and teacher of Indigos.

Charles: As an Indigo myself, born in 1978, I can relate to what other Indigos are going through. I've been teaching about spirituality around the world since 2007. I also want to take the painful experiences of my life and turn them around into positive learning opportunities for others.

This book is our conversation, as a mother and as an Indigo son, of what it's like to be Indigo . . . and the blessings this remarkable generation brings to us all. It's *Indigo Power*, which we *all* can awaken within ourselves.

Part I

WHAT WE CAN ALL LEARN FROM THE INDIGOS

RECOGNIZE THAT YOU HAVE AN IMPORTANT MISSION ONLY YOU CAN FULFILL

Throughout history, Indigos have owned their power, as we'll explore in this book. They have defied the rules and forged their own pathways to positive change. Many risked their lives or their reputations, and some even *sacrificed* their lives for their mission.

The majority of Indigos were born in the 1970s, because the world needed their Indigo Power at that time. It was an era when U.S. President Nixon resigned his office after being caught in a criminal scandal. This burst everyone's bubble that the commander-in-chief was above reproach.

This rude awakening to reality, hard on the heels of the Vietnam War, left people feeling cynical and betrayed. The '60s and '70s were a time of massive social change, calling for fairness for minorities. Widespread drug use, rock-and-roll music, and free love were ways that teens and young adults released their frustrations.

Indigos born to these parents are among the members of Generation X, who are often labeled "slackers" or "self-absorbed." There's a crossover and a distinction between Generation X and Indigos, in that Indigos are born highly intuitive and Gen X–ers, also born in the 1970s, aren't necessarily intuitive.

Doreen: As I explained in my book *The Care and Feeding of Indigo Children*:

> The term *Indigo Children* refers to the color "indigo blue," which is a deep shade of blue similar to that found in lapis stones or denim jeans. The term is derived from *chakra*, or energy, colors. Each generation seems to have a group consciousness—a group purpose, if you will. We can relate each generation's adult years to an issue and a correlated chakra, along with its corresponding color.
>
> For instance, those in the post-Depression and post–World War II eras of the 1940s and 1950s had issues of *security*. They married young and stayed at their jobs for a lifetime. Happiness in their marriage or career was secondary to the security afforded by their stations. This type of outlook is akin to the "root chakra," which is an energy center located at the base of the spine.
>
> Each chakra spins at a different rate, according to what issues are assigned to that chakra. The chakras assigned to material issues spin at a slower rate than the more spiritually focused chakras.
>
> As you may know, when light moves slowly, it is perceived as the "warm colors," such as red, orange, and yellow. The faster that light waves move, the cooler their colors are. Purple is the highest-speed color, and is also associated with the most spiritual of frequencies. . . .

> Interest in psychic phenomena is regulated by the sixth chakra, known as the "third eye." This chakra spins at three different colors: white, purple, and primarily *indigo*.
>
> Children who were born in the mid-1970s through the present day are often called Indigo Children because they are, literally, "children of the indigo ray."[1]

What we see is that both Gen X–ers and Indigos are angry and upset at the world. The Indigos, though, are the people who feel an inner sense of duty to *do* something about the problems they see.

Indigos who understand their personal power are using their gifts to positively change the world. You can do the same by studying Indigo Power in yourself and in others.

When we get in touch with our Indigo Power, and then channel it constructively, we become agents of change:

- Documentary film directors
- Inventors and innovators
- Leaders, coaches, and teachers
- Bloggers, vloggers, and social commentators
- Activists
- Artists
- Environmentalists
- Authors
- Animal-rights spokespeople
- Speakers
- Charity volunteers

The possibilities are endless for channeling anger and frustration in positive ways.

Indigo Activism

A modern-day example is Julia "Butterfly" Hill, who lived in a massive 180-foot tree for over two years in the 1990s, while in her early 20s, to protect it from being chopped down. Can you imagine this dedication to saving trees, which compelled Julia to live on a small platform suspended between branches?

Even though she was threatened with civil disobedience fines or worse, she stuck to her principles. Although angry loggers confronted and threatened her daily, Julia stayed in the tree. Meanwhile, other activists helped her by hoisting supplies to her using ropes, and the situation received lots of media attention.

At the end of 738 days, the logging company backed down and agreed to leave the tree, which Julia had affectionately named "Luna." Since this time, Julia continues to channel her Indigo Power into environmentalism with her books and speeches.

Sometimes our egos argue with us that we need to be older or have more schooling in order to make a positive difference. Julia is a prime example that anyone at any age, without a higher degree, can step up to leadership.

Is this arrogance or misguided magical thinking to believe one individual can stand up to many? History tells us that the original thinkers were the pioneering trailblazers ushering in positive change.

Think of Dr. Martin Luther King, Jr., an early Indigo who paved the way to racial reform and equality. At the age of 26, Dr. King led a boycott of buses in Montgomery, Alabama, to protest segregation. At that time, buses required that African Americans sit in the back. Isn't that unbelievable to think of now? But then no one dared to question segregation . . . except for young Dr. King and his circle of activists—including Rosa Parks, who had been arrested for refusing to give up her bus seat to a Caucasian rider.

He persuaded other African Americans to join the boycott so the bus company would realize how much money they were losing with segregation. The boycotters suffered during this demonstration, having to walk long distances to work and such. But Dr. King rallied everyone, convincing them to not relent until the bus company treated them equally. And it worked!

After a yearlong boycott, the United States Supreme Court ruled that bus segregation was unconstitutional. Dr. King and his supporters channeled their anger constructively to make a statement.

(Boycotting is still a highly effective form of nonviolent resistance, by the way, and the world needs leaders like you to step up and speak up.)

Indigo Gifts

Indigo Children, more recently known simply as the "Indigos," are blessed souls of Heaven, just like everyone— but with a collective life purpose to bring positive change to our world with their unique spiritual gifts.

Indigos are naturally highly tuned in to the etheric energy around them. Many parents report that their young Indigo Children have a natural and inherent ability to see and communicate with the angels.

Not only that, but it's widely understood that Indigo Children have natural mediumship abilities. This means that Indigos are attuned to communication with the souls that were once in human bodies who now serve as spirit guides for humanity.

Charles: Another one of the amazing tools that Indigos are bestowed with is the power of instinct or gut feeling. When there is a truth present that's not spoken, they are aware of it. They are always able to see through any given situation to the core dynamics.

Now this is usually a very automatic process that most Indigos do not have to put any thought into. They just *know* when something is not right. But a lot of Indigos don't realize how much more they could be doing with their instinct if they learned to make healthier choices— to take care of themselves better and value themselves more highly, to stop beating themselves up and start having more confidence in who they are not only as people but also as soul warriors.

As we all bring that energy up, our intuition grows clearer and clearer and more and more automatic. This is something we can use every day of our lives.

The Life Purpose of Indigos

Indigos are often "old souls" who have waited for this Divine time of human awakening and evolution to return here to Earth. These evolved beings seem to hit the ground running with a mission as soon as they're born and consistently display common characteristics of being very aware, sensitive, and intuitive.

The Indigos are here for one major purpose: to open our eyes to the world around us so that we can recognize the much-needed and important changes that must be made. The Indigo spirit has always existed among humankind but is more noticeable now than ever before in recorded history.

It is beyond debate that humanity is "waking up" all around the globe, and with this new awareness, we are realizing just how outdated and control based many institutions have become.

We all want change, and in the past a violent revolution was often thought necessary to bring it about. But those days are over, and now Heaven is working more closely with humanity to enact positive change. In this regard, we are being blessed with the unstoppable will of the Indigo.

Indigos can be considered *angels* of change, because they come into life with a great, Heavenly mission to question rules, authority, and dogma, as we will discuss in the next chapter. The Indigos shine light upon dishonesty to make us review and analyze our world, and to actually put thought into our daily actions and goals.

Indigo energy—although commonly associated with behavioral issues, so it seems counterintuitive—is a *higher-vibrational* energy than just regular, everyday human energy.

Indigos are often called the *new* or the *gifted children*, because they come here with such a high purpose. Purpose can be anything—it could be to become the parent of beautiful children or start a company to give people jobs or simply be a great contributor to society or perpetrator of good. With a purpose on the scale of changing the face of civilization on an entire planet, though, these souls are obviously going to resonate with a much higher energy than that of most people because of the spiritual magnitude of their task.

Discerning Your Life Purpose

Charles: Now if you are feeling lost and confused about what it is that you can do in this world to make a difference, what your unique soul-chosen role is, we want to share with you some secrets on how you can get in tune with your life purpose.

One method that a lot of Indigos have great success with is automatic writing. Grab a pen and a piece of paper, or you can even do this at your computer. With a blank document in front of you, either electronic or physical, just write down the first thing that comes to you.

> *Close your eyes and take a deep breath. Let your-self feel peaceful and calm; allow any stress or intense emotions you might be experiencing or any thoughts racing through your mind to escape from you through your exhale.*
>
> *Just take a moment to be aware of the entire world, the entire universe, and all the energy within this plane of existence. Think about the fact that you came here with a Divine role, with a Divine pur-pose to fulfill. Then ask the universe, this energy that's around you:* How can I help the world? . . . How can I help the world?
>
> *Trust your instinct and write down whatever comes to you. No matter what you think of it—no matter how outlandish or ridiculous it seems—just write down the first thing you see, think, hear, feel. Write whatever you are guided to, without censoring it.*

Do this consistently. Whenever you find yourself won-dering, *What am I supposed to do with my life? What am I supposed to do in this world?* keep a journal of what comes through. Write something down on a new piece of paper or new electronic document every time.

After a little while—a couple of weeks or months—read through the notes and look for consistencies, because your body, your energy, knows why you came here. If you put regular effort into channeling these messages through, you are going to find an answer—just like that.

Doreen: As I described in *The Care and Feeding of Indigo Children*, here are the four main categories related to the life purpose of Indigos:

— *The Healer.* Your life purpose involves helping people or animals heal their physical bodies. You might do this through conventional healing means (such as being a doctor, nurse, or veterinarian) or through alternative means (such as acupuncture, herbology, crystal healing, and so on).

— *The Teacher/Healer.* Your life purpose involves teaching people, which has a healing effect upon them or others. For instance, you might teach healing methods to other healers or teach people how to heal themselves. You might write healing books or give workshops about healing methods.

— *The Messenger.* This person helps the world through their communication talents. Their work could be in the form of creative pursuits that bring joy to the world, such as music, painting, photography, cooking, dance, decorating, designing, or acting. Many Messengers also go into the media, such as television, radio, newspaper, magazines, or blogging. They also make wonderful counselors (especially if they have the gift of gab), researchers, and schoolteachers.

— *The Energy Worker.* Some people have bands of colors, like a rainbow, surrounding their bodies. Or the bands of color may emanate from the open palms of their hands. This life purpose involves hands-on healing work, or energy healing. They find true happiness and success in being a physical therapist, chiropractor, massage therapist, Reiki master, or pranic healer.

You can discern whether you fit into these categories by answering *yes* or *no* to the following questions:

1. *Do strangers tend to pour their hearts out to me and tell me their problems?*

2. *Do people say to me, "There's something about you that seems so familiar, like I've known you forever"?*

3. *Do I find myself teaching other people how to improve their lives?*

4. *Do I often give advice that is so wise that I wonder where those ideas came from (a "Who said that?" kind of experience)?*

5. *Do my friends constantly call on me for encouragement, comfort, and advice?*

6. *Do I love to read books or articles?*

7. *Do I sometimes practice speaking or singing in front of the mirror?*

8. *Do I seem to have a natural artistic gift?*

9. *Do I love to create and make things?*

10. *Am I constantly starting new projects that I never seem to quite complete?*

11. *When I put my hands on someone's shoulders, back, or stomach, do they remark how wonderful it makes them feel?*

12. *Do my friends and family members constantly ask me to give them massages?*

13. *Do I love to receive massages myself and often massage my own hands, feet, or scalp?*

14. *Have I intuitively known how to "send healing energy" to a person or an animal, and felt that it had positive results?*

15. *Do watches tend to stop working when I wear them, or do other electrical items (lights, televisions sets, radios, phones, and so on) tend to act funny or break in my presence?*

16. *Do I feel like I would be, or could have been, a great doctor?*

17. *Do I seem to have a natural ability to know what babies want when they're crying or what animals need when they're sick?*

18. *Am I fascinated with learning about new healing techniques?*

19. *Do I have a history of childhood illness?*

20. *Do I have a sense, or a calling, that I could help other people or animals live healthier and longer lives?*

Interpreting your answers: Notice which of the categories you had the most affirmative answers in, and then read the description of that life-purpose category on the preceding pages.

Questions 1–5: If most of your *yes* answers were in this group of questions, you're a Teacher/Healer.

Questions 6–10: If most of your *yes* answers were in this group of questions, you're a Messenger.

Questions 11–15: If most of your *yes* answers were in this group of questions, you're an Energy Worker.

Questions 16–20: If most of your *yes* answers were in this group of questions, you're a Healer.

Indigo Power takeaway:

The Indigos teach us to honor our own individuality and uniqueness. Know that you—like all of us—are exactly who you are for a Divine reason. You have an important mission that only you can fulfill. If you try to be like everyone else, you will block your mission, as well as your happiness and fulfillment.

LESSON 2

QUESTION EVERYTHING— INCLUDING THE "RULES"

Indigos can be any age; however, the majority were born in the 1970s. This was an era of lost innocence.

Prior to the 1960s and '70s, there was an innocent or naïve trust within most people. If a popular actor starred in a commercial, then the advertised product must be good. If a chart at school said to eat lots of meat, butter, and cheese every day for your health, then it must be true. If someone wore a uniform, they were certainly an honest person. Everything was taken at face value.

The post–Vietnam War and Watergate era awakened suspicion and disillusionment in many people, and the motto was "Question Authority." How Indigo is that?

Indigos, Rules, and Societal Expectations

Indigos, like everyone, have an inner truth detector. It's that gut feeling that senses whether something is valid or not. It's the ability to feel a harmony or disharmony, letting you know if you can trust someone or not.

What sets the Indigos born in the 1970s or later apart is that they *trust their gut feelings*. They live by their inner compass.

This means that if an "authority figure" such as a teacher, principal, or parent imposes a rule, the first thing an Indigo does is check their gut feelings about it. Unless the Indigo understands the reason behind the rule, they will not follow it.

Indigos also scan the energy of the authority figure imposing the rule to determine whether they respect the person or not. Indigos will only abide by rules if they understand and agree with them, and if the rule makers garner their respect.

Indigos never met a rule they couldn't break. After all, Indigos have a group purpose to teach and model being limitless.

An *evolved* Indigo who is consciously aware of their own inner processes, and who strives to live ethically, will express limitlessness in healthy ways. They do seemingly impossible yoga poses; they dream up logic-defying business ideas that help us all . . . and become highly successful. The evolved Indigo radiates an abundance mentality and refuses to be held back by fear.

The *unaware* Indigo is just angry about rules, and lashes out without a plan. They live by the motto "It's easier to beg for forgiveness later than ask for permission first." This type of Indigo becomes sneaky, which doesn't feel good to them.

Some Indigos see themselves as complete anarchists who annihilate all rules. Fortunately, the "Let's smash the system apart" movement has evolved into a more methodical approach. Instead of adopting a blind-rage attitude of "Let's overtake the government," Indigos are now thinking things through. They look at one problem at a time and then offer solutions.

The Not-So-Clear Purpose of the Clearly Guided Indigo

The particular Indigo spirit in our world today has been defined in many ways. Some consider it to be a rebellious, socially disadvantaged condition; others see it as a sign that parenting and caretaking are so detached that discipline has become a secondary concern. Some people think the Indigo spirit is a chemical imbalance that can easily be resolved a few milligrams at a time. But no matter what people think of these blessed souls, they definitely *notice* them.

Besides these behavioral views, though, there is another: that these children are Heaven-sent warriors meant to wake us up to the imbalanced, impractical, outdated, and unethical aspects of modern-day life.

Indeed, Indigo Children are guided by Heaven to question the rules and practices humans often turn a blind eye to. Since humanity is a pretty complacent species, it is no surprise that something within us had to change in order for us to collectively seek a different way of life.

Indigo Inquisitiveness

Indigos are here as old souls because they have nothing more to learn from our world the way it's currently designed. They come across as wise, enlightened, intelligent, and advanced simply because they've been through this process of incarnation so many times before. Their souls have reached the point of saturation, where another ordinary life, just another humdrum existence, would teach them absolutely nothing. So they've taken it upon themselves to come back with this extra sense of rebellion.

As you talk about history, about "facts," they're not going to simply take your word for it and accept it and believe it just because you say it.

They're not going to passively allow knowledge to be transmitted to them without thinking about it, without asking detailed questions, without looking for supporting information. You'll notice that this personality trait—the need to know why—applies to many different aspects of working with Indigos. They're constantly asking very probing questions about the world around them.

This can sometimes be exhausting and overwhelming for caretakers. But we have to understand that their entire purpose is not just about asking questions for their own sake, or disobeying rules to satisfy an inner sense of rebellion. Their purpose is to act as a mirror to help the *world* understand why things are the way they are.

We have a responsibility to explain ourselves; we need to justify our rules andexplain to them *why* they have to fall in line.

When we actually do that—when instead of just regurgitating and passing on these rules and policies, we actually take the time to think about them—that's when we realize for ourselves what is wrong with our world, what is outmoded, what is just being perpetuated for the sake of tradition . . . all the things we do that we don't really put thought into, that we just do because other humans are doing them.

Real change in this world is going to come from us all being truly aware of what works for us and what no longer works for us.

Charles: I am convinced it will be the Indigo energy that will eventually rid us of rush-hour traffic. Think about it: If you ever sit in rush-hour traffic, how happy are you? If you actually look out the window at the other people sitting there with you, how happy are *they*? Is this what we all envisioned for our lives—that we collectively decide at a certain time to get on a narrow band of asphalt, then grow upset that we are all here and allow that energy to follow us home?

One day, during the peak of stop-and-go traffic, an Indigo is going to get out of their car and say, "I am not doing this anymore; this isn't necessary. There is no force that's compelling us all to sit on this road in a manner that is proven every day to be inefficient. None of us enjoys this. Yet we mindlessly repeat this ritual every single day, and we are victims of our own collective decision to do so."

So when we all wake up to what doesn't work for us—when somebody actually leads the parade—we can understand how the Indigo energy can make changes, like adopting a traffic tier system, to redesign society.

Instead of sitting complacently, we can all get out of our cars and decide to design something better.

Rebelling for Peace?

To impose a rule upon an Indigo, you must explain its nature and *raison d'être*—its purpose for being—in order for the Indigo to understand. This may feel like a lot of work, but the Indigos are forcing us to take inventory of our planet and the way of life that we have created. When so much light is shed upon our day-to-day lives, we are prompted to see through it all and discover what is working for us and what no longer resonates with our modern-day desires.

That is the principal essence of the Indigo spirit: The world does not resonate with our modern-day desires. Too many people feel like outcasts, at odds with our sometimes cold and competitive ways. And in order for true peace to exist on this planet, we have to wake up and allow ourselves to become more empathetic toward our fellow humans.

Heaven-Sent Warriors

Now you may be asking yourself, *How can rambunctious youths inspire world peace?* You'd be right to wonder, but please allow me to explain. In order for a true warrior spirit to survive the assimilation processes of upbringing, they must have an unbreakable spirit.

Indigos epitomize this; no amount of medication or harsh discipline can take away their inherent need to question and dissect authority. As these children grow into adults, their natural ability to detect truth in their surroundings often guides them to make a difference. We can see evidence of the Indigo spirit almost every day in the news; many civilizations, after thousands of years of the same type of rule, are finally putting their foot down and demanding change.

You can see it with the youth-led revolutions that are happening. While these uprisings have always occurred in human society throughout history, right now especially, in the face of these totalitarian governments with oppressive regimes, people are just standing out in the street and saying, "This no longer works for me. This is no longer the reality that I feel resonates with me, and I am not going to take it anymore."

As Indigos age and integrate with society, their inquisitive and sometimes stubborn ways change the elements of almost every industry they join. What is right and fair assumes priority in the view of the Indigo, and a "people before profit" strategy begins to take hold.

While not all Indigos are always open to spiritual topics at first, it is important to remind them that they do have a very powerful purpose on this planet; and although they so often feel totally out of place, time will reveal to them just how essential they are to the world. Since they tend to amplify the energy they experience, we must remember that harsh reactions will only perpetuate the negativity we may be attempting to curtail.

Indigo Survival Guide

Charles: I used to get in trouble a lot when I was young, which bothered me. So I analyzed what was going on. I felt stuck for a long time, because I didn't like the rules or find them logical. I asked myself how I could ever fit in. Then I was sitting outside one day when I had an epiphany: I don't have to like or agree with the rules; I just need to play by them. It was such a profound realization that I started laughing and saw how it's all just a game—and this changed my life.

Indigos have a Heavenly mission, let's not forget that. I do understand, however, that day-to-day life must go on—and we all know deep down that a certain amount of obedience is required to get through it. I find that one of the most important and empowering things you can do for an Indigo is relate to them, listen to what is upsetting them. When they are willing to share their thoughts, you'll find a surprising receptiveness to reason.

You cannot impose general, blanket rules on these individuals without a clear explanation as to why they are necessary. They may still question the rule, but over time and with your continued support, they will eventually realize, like I did, that life is sort of a game, and certain norms must be followed in order for them to get what they want.

Of course, for an Indigo, it's still tough to get your act together when you don't understand the "rules" of a dysfunctional planet.

Well, here are a few tips to give you the ropes of Earth living in the 21st century:

— **Learn to deal.** So the world's not perfect, and people are disappointing . . . learn to deal with it, and make life the best that you can. Instead of complaining about problems, put your focus into pledging to solve them. Everyone is struggling with problems; you're not the only one.

— **Know that you're never too young.** You can make a positive difference, run a business, write a best-selling book, and accomplish anything that you're guided to do, even at a super young age. In fact, sometimes projects go *better* when you're younger because people are charmed by your youthfulness. They want to help you . . . so please do allow yourself to be helped, mentored, and supported.

— Yes, money is a drag for everyone, but accept that this method of exchange is the way it is for now. The whole money system seems archaic and unfair to everyone, and someday we'll move to a more efficient system. But for right now, the money system is the way that it is. Unless you're prepared to live off the land or you are financially independent, you'll need to create an income. Sometimes, that means working in a job that you don't like. Fortunately, you can start your own business or partner with other visionaries to make your work more meaningful (a topic we'll explore in Lesson 6).

Indigo Power takeaway:

The Indigos empower us to question everything and not accept rules just because some perceived "authority figure" issues them.

LESSON 3

BE TRUE TO HOW YOU FEEL, AND CHANNEL EMOTIONS IN POSITIVE WAYS

Anger and frustration are Indigo characteristics that can seem problematic at first glance. However, health-conscious Indigos teach us that this energy can be channeled in positive ways.

Perhaps you feel angry and frustrated, too. Everyone does at times. Yet when anger is stuffed down instead of honestly addressed, it can lead to depression, addictive behavior, and health challenges.

What are Indigos *angry* about? A lot of things, including corporate greed; unethical political decisions and actions; war; exploitation of people, animals, and the environment; cruelty; inequality in the economic system; and dishonesty.

What are Indigos *frustrated* about? That other people can't see what they clearly can (that is, corruption and the toxic path being taken) and aren't doing anything to stop the crazy destructiveness. That people are focusing upon shallow entertainment issues, instead of what really matters.

The mistreatment of other people, animals, and the environment are issues that are upsetting to nearly everyone; however, most try to block out awareness of them. They hide upsetting stories from their news feed and click elsewhere when someone posts a photo showing the truth.

Indigos lack the option to turn off awareness of these issues, because they can feel and sense the energies of current events way before they're posted on social media. Ultra-empaths, Indigos are *bombarded* by their awareness.

Like warriors and superheroes, the Indigos feel that it's their mission to teach, way-show, whistle-blow, avenge, and take charge of what's going on in the world . . . since it's obvious to them that most leaders are self-serving.

Indigos and Anger

When you're angered by a situation, you basically have three choices:

1. Look the other way and pretend it doesn't exist, thus stuffing down your anger, which usually results in feelings of helplessness or depression.

2. Do something destructive to express your anger (for example, acting out with violence, either toward others or self-inflicted).

3. Do something constructive to help (intervening directly, for instance, or educating others).

Indigos don't have the ability to opt for Choice #1. They cannot turn off awareness, unless they are heavily medicated (by prescription or illicitly). To an Indigo, when you're angry, it's Choice #2 or Choice #3. Indigos who are conscientious and own their power elect to go for Choice #3—and they are changing the world in the process.

The key is authenticity and being honest with yourself about your feelings. Don't judge yourself for being angry . . . *do* something about it.

For example, Gabriela Cowperthwaite was upset when she read about a SeaWorld trainer's drowning, apparently due to an attack by the orca she had been training. Gabriela intuitively felt there was more to the story. She had taken her children to see the killer-whale shows at Sea-World and wanted to know the truth.

The need to ferret out the truth is almost an obsession with Indigos, who only feel settled by understanding what's really going on. In Gabriela's words, she "unfortunately can't let sleeping dogs lie." She *has* to expose the truth.

So Gabriela began talking to various experts and soon discovered the perils of keeping cetaceans in captivity. She decided to make a documentary film called *Blackfish*, which went on to win awards and alert others to the cruelty and hazards of whale captivity.

During the making of the film, Gabriela was well aware that she was upsetting a multibillion-dollar corporation, but she defied the danger and expressed her anger through an influential film. Because of *Blackfish*, millions of viewers became educated about the plight of captive cetaceans, and attendance at SeaWorld and similar venues plummeted.

Although Indigos can be any age, it is interesting to note how many of those born in the '70s (Gabriela was born in 1971) are now channeling their Indigo Power into world-changing products and services.

The Indigo Expression of Anger

Indigos express their "rage against the machine" in different ways.

Fashion Style

The gothic and spiked-accessory looks are the Indigos' way of saying, "I refuse to fit in with a society I don't believe in." Indigos think that sugary sweetness in fashion or manner is fake and insincere, so they dress as a reflection of how they feel on the inside: dark, edgy, and angry.

Indigos seem fascinated with skull imagery, not so much to emulate pirates, but more as a display that they're fearless. Wearing a skull is an Indigo symbol of being tough and hardened by life.

An Indigo won't dress to fit in, to impress others, or to pretend to be different. Indigos express their frustration in innovative ways—with shaved, spiked, and chalked hair; piercings; tattoos; and "goth" clothing. As soon as these fashions become popularized, the Indigo changes to something new. Being mainstream is against the Indigo's sensibilities.

Some Indigos choose eco-friendly clothing as their expression of anger about the environmental impact of synthetic fabrics and chemical dyes. Increasingly, young fashion designers are opting for organic fabrics, low-impact dyes, and fair-trade labor for the creation of their clothing. A group of students who were concerned about the cruel treatment of sweatshop garment workers channeled their emotions into creating a charity called United Students Against Sweatshops. They raise awareness about conscious clothing choices.

We've also noticed that as Indigos become parents themselves, they buy or make organic clothing for their children. Favorite fabric choices for Indigos are organic cotton, hemp, or true bamboo (some bamboo is blended with polyester) with low-impact fabric dyes. Indigos, being extra-sensitive to chemicals, don't want to expose their children to toxins.

Music Choices

Youth cultures have used music as a way of expressing their feelings for many generations, and the Indigo generation is no different.

Soundgarden, Pearl Jam, and Nirvana are iconic bands, symbols of the anger and dissociation of the Indigo generation as the majority of 1970s-born Indigos entered young adulthood during the grunge era of the late 1980s and early '90s.

This was also the time when the hard-rock music of the 1970s and glam rock of the 1980s morphed into death-metal music of the 1990s, by using morbid and gruesome lyrics with screeching lead singers.

The fascination with death-metal music may have sprung from the Indigos feeling hopeless regarding this world and their lives. Death metal reflects the angst they feel within. This relates to the skull image fashion trend of the 1990s, too. A focus upon death may be a fantasy about escaping.

Doreen: As I wrote in my book *Don't Let Anything Dull Your Sparkle*:

> A comparison of people listening to either classical music, heavy-metal music, or no music found that classical music resulted in measurable calming effects . . . but silence and heavy metal did not. Studies show that anxiety and blood pressure are significantly reduced in those who listen to classical or meditation music prior to a stressful event (such as surgery). . . .
>
> Cardiovascular patients showed so much improvement in heart rate while they listened to relaxing music, according to studies, that researchers recommended playing music bedside while people recover from heart surgery. The lead researcher concluded:
>
>> The greatest benefit on health is visible with classical music and meditation music, whereas heavy metal music or techno are not only ineffective but possibly dangerous and can lead to stress and/or life-threatening arrhythmias. The music of many composers most effectively improves quality of life, will increase health and probably prolong life. (Trappe 2010).
>
> . . . So, be discerning with regard to the music you listen to, as it affects your mood and energy. I highly recommend playing calming music as a way of reducing anxiety.[1]

Charles: Even if you feel that you relate to the music on a personal level and it speaks to the problems in your life, it's important to know that listening to that sort of music isn't helping you. It only perpetuates and compounds the issues that you feel upset about. It keeps you stuck. Listening to music that only reflects your sad and upsetting feelings is like complaining to a friend repeatedly about your problems. No solutions come from it. You just stay wallowing in the sorrow and anger, and don't move on.

The Indigo fascination with death and Armageddon can be expressed as a wish for it. Some are afraid that the end of the world *is* upon us, so they wonder, *Why bother?* That's why a spiritual path can help Indigos have faith that everything happens for a reason, even if we don't know or understand it. Spirituality can help Indigos relax and make peace with the craziness of the world.

Video Games

Video gaming is an outlet for Indigo frustration. Games serve two purposes:

1. **Entertainment and escape**. When you enter the world of a video game, you can temporarily forget about your earthly troubles. You also escape boredom, because games offer adrenaline-pumping excitement.

2. **Social connection**. Many games are played in virtual groups on gaming sites, meaning that you are playing with others remotely. The electronic connection with others during games leads to cyber friendships, which can fill the void of loneliness in Indigos. It can feel like a safe option if you have social anxieties.

Indigos need to watch their escapism through video gaming, especially as new video-game technology (such as virtual reality) emerges. There can be a split in consciousness and identity, where you have two lives.

While video games give you a sense of purpose and belonging, at the end of the day they're not real life. You've accomplished nothing unless you have a future in video-game design or programming.

The violence in video games can bring Indigos' energy down and can make some more aggressive. Violent and intense video games can increase Indigos' impulsivity and lead to social withdrawal. There are nonviolent video-game options, especially for those who have suffered a traumatic experience that makes them hypervigilant and anxious.

In our experience, Indigos seem drawn toward violent video games. Perhaps there's something cathartic about expressing your frustration through a virtual avatar who does your bidding for you. But there's also a highly addictive component to video gaming. The video games are addictive because there's no end to the game story line, and you can forget to take care of your physical needs.

The research on video gaming has found that playing violent video games increases aggressive thoughts and behaviors in those who were already predisposed to violence. Those without a violent predisposition may not be influenced to become so. However, it appears that engaging in virtual violence can makes people desensitized and less compassionate when violence appears in real life.

There is concern from research about people becoming addicted to playing video games—to the exclusion of developing in-person friendships. Some researchers believe that video gaming can lead to antisocial personality development. There have also been extreme instances of people neglecting their physical needs for food, water, and urinating while they were gaming—to the detriment of their health.

However, there's also positive research showing that video games can enhance motor skills and hand-eye coordination.

We believe that nonviolent video games, played in moderation, can be a pleasant pastime for Indigos . . . provided that the games don't interfere with self-care, work or school, and real-life relationships.

The Dark Side of Indigo Anger

You'll notice that there are light and dark sides to each aspect of Indigo Power, and that includes anger especially.

Indigos can feel the pain in the world around them, and we see their reaction to this pain expressed as anxiety, moody temperament, and sometimes seclusion—but ultimately they mirror the energy they encounter. When an Indigo is happy, you simply cannot find a more enjoyable person to be around, and when they are upset . . . watch out, as their anger energy is a force of nature.

Rays of Hope—for Indigos and Caretakers

Charles: I talk with a lot of parents whose Indigo Children are facing legal problems or severe discipline problems in school. Perhaps they're getting kicked out or have gotten kicked out. All that such rejection does is perpetuate their anger and make the Indigo feel worse about themselves.

Oftentimes I'm asked, "What can I do? How can I work with my child who is going though these legal problems and has really big issues with rage?"

Parents feel that their children are totally turning their backs on them, and no matter what they do, they can't seem to get through to them.

It's not always easy because, again, there's not one pat answer as to how to deal with someone who is rebelling. I maintain that one of the most important things a parent can do is watch their own energy.

It's become socially acceptable and expected to react with disappointment, anger, or some form of discipline when a child misbehaves. While I would never want to get inside someone's head and make parental decisions for them, heightened compassion, even if we're angry, is going to get us further with Indigos, even if we feel that the traditional reactions are more appropriate.

That's not to say that the Indigo deserves special treatment, but just try out compassion. Experiment with this as a parent or caretaker, and see the result.

When we react with anger, we serve to compound the issues that created the bad behavior in the first place. As unpleasant as that can be to hear, it is the truth.

We need to understand the truth of Indigos. We need to work with them in the context of discipline to help them understand—to explain to them exactly how and why their actions are affecting their future, and why it's so important.

When we can adopt a more constructive, helpful, and peer-like role in the way that we work to correct their behavior, we're going to experience Indigos that are more responsive to our reactions. That's just the truth of it.

If you sit an Indigo down and spell out for them exactly how their behavior is going to affect their future—if you can help them believe that they actually *have* a future—then you're going to make much more progress.

The truth is, a lot of young Indigos feel there is no hope. The level of carelessness with which they act reflects their belief that the future holds no promise for them.

It's difficult for an Indigo to value what is important in modern-day society—to respect the rules, to respect authority, to respect parents—because they don't *believe* in the world the way it is today.

They look at the whole, as opposed to the parts. In the face of the magnitude of change the planet requires, it's difficult for them to respect *any* aspect of a world they don't see themselves ever having a role in.

If you entered into a conversation with an Indigo with behavioral issues, you'd realize that they can't even *imagine* how they could ever fit into this world. They don't want to. They have no interest in being a part of it.

They don't aspire to things like getting a job that they would just "default" into, and surviving every day solely to be able to afford the newest Apple *this* or the latest Windows *that*. These incentives don't have enough meaning to motivate an Indigo to fall in line.

That's why I spend so much time underlining the benefit of leveling with an Indigo. Explaining to them, "Look, understand that the world is a game, and you've got to just play it. You don't have to believe in it. You don't have to like it; just play along." Trust me, Indigos have more than enough intelligence and sophistication to grasp this concept.

Help Indigos understand that if they can just play the game, the world will get easier for them to exist in. They don't have to believe in it. They can still make changes. They can still make a difference, even if they have gotten in trouble.

Even if they feel that they've potentially ruined or affected some level of their future, they have to understand that it's never too late. *It's never too late.*

No matter what they've done—no matter how bad they may feel or how upset they may be—life is long. There are a lot of opportunities to start over—to still follow their dreams and come to believe that they can eventually find their place in the world.

One thing that I've experienced, not only in my own life but also with so many people I've talked to about their Indigo Children, is that the energy does eventually settle down. That's not to say that their Indigo nature goes away, but their need and their constant desire to resist the world around them and the rules that they experience so harshly does begin to lessen.

It's really important for all caretakers of Indigo Children to be aware of this truth, because we tend to not only think about the present but also project into the future. A lot of parents worry about where this behavior will lead. *If my child is doing this now, what comes next?*

We assume that if a child is acting bad now, it could only get worse, and we may actually experience some evidence of that. Maybe they start acting out in their early teens, and then in their later teens, they're kicked out of school. Then our minds default to our belief that as they grow older and become adults, their actions are just going to be more self-destructive or dangerous.

The good news is that Indigo energy does naturally begin to calm after the adolescent years. Most Indigos are going to experience a level of natural peace—enough so that they can act as contributing members of our society.

Behavioral issues arise in large part as a result of the reaction the behavior receives. That's not to say that it's anyone's fault. It's no one's fault, and once again, I want to underscore that I'm not implying Indigos deserve special treatment. (After all, compassion and calmness benefit everyone.)

However, I will qualify that by serving up a reminder that the clearer and more specific caretakers, parents, and teachers of Indigos can be, the further they're going to get in their efforts to work with these children—and talk them into acting more in accordance with societal norms and expectations.

Indigo Health Consciousness

On top of the energy Indigos are exposed to—as far as social situations, disciplinary actions, and school settings go—it's also very important to be aware of what substances and nourishment they're putting into their bodies.

Yet again, there is no one-size-fits-all solution, no magic cure for Indigo anger and defiance (nor should we even consider Indigos to be in need of "curing"). After all, you've likely seen a video on social media of a young person passionately ranting about world problems . . . and you've probably admired him or her on some level for head-on confronting the truth. Such videos normally go viral, because we all recognize the innate leadership and truth-telling of the young person.

You also see Indigo Power at work with people who stand up to powerful corporations. For example, a young mother in California named Zen Honeycutt searched for answers as to why her three sons all had allergies and autistic symptoms.

When she learned that glyphosate (a pesticide/herbicide marketed as Roundup) was correlated with both autism and allergies, Zen had her sons' urine tested. She was horrified that her middle son's urine had eight times more glyphosate than is allowed in European drinking water.

So Zen eliminated all genetically modified food (which is sprayed with and contains glyphosate) from her family's meals and switched to organic food. Within six weeks, the glyphosate had left her sons' systems.

Most impressively, her sons' allergies and autism symptoms were greatly reduced. Inspired, Zen set out to raise awareness for other parents. She channeled her passion for detoxifying family meals into creating an activism charity called Moms Across America, which organizes marches, delivers speeches, and posts billboards, lobbying to eliminate glyphosate from America (it is banned in many places in the world).

Zen exhibits Indigo Power bravery by speaking at shareholder meetings at Monsanto and other corporations that profit from making and selling glyphosate. Now that takes a lot of courage, and that's Indigo Power! You can read more about Zen's activism on her Twitter page (@yesmaam74) and website (MomsAcrossAmerica.com).

Moodiness and Irritability

Indigos often complain about feeling angry and irritable. In our interviews, they say the source of their upset is other people. They're indignant about world events and annoyed that people are being dishonest or passive.

This results in Indigos feeling restless, depressed, or anxious. It's a bad mood that comes from extreme disappointment in the human race.

To an Indigo, it's disingenuous to pretend you're happy when you're not—it's fake, in other words. So Indigos wear their bad moods on their sleeves. If an Indigo is in a bad mood, you (and everyone else) will know it. Some Indigos turn to addictions to numb their emotional pain. However, addictions only work temporarily and actually lead to increased irritability in the long run.

Since Indigos don't have the ability to cover their feelings or pretend they're happy, conversations and other interactions can be strained, tense, or argumentative.

Parents who blame themselves for their Indigo's unhappiness may nosedive into guilt or codependency. This means that the parent may try to control the Indigo, to coerce happiness to happen. The Indigo doesn't want to be pushed to comply, though. This can result in a power struggle between parent and child, and may push the Indigo away.

Here are some ways that Indigos can manage their anger and still stay true to themselves:

— **Shift focus from the external to the internal.** Saying "I can't be happy until people change" gives away your power to others. Going through life angry does not improve life situations—it actually contributes more anger to the world. Instead, be a role model who inspires others to live at a higher level. Take care of your inner world through self-care measures such as meditating, yoga, and organic food. As your light then shines, others will notice and be inspired to become more conscious too.

— **Channel anger in positive, constructive ways.** Use the powerful energy of anger to take positive constructive action. For example, join or start a charitable organization to help with issues that upset you. Create, sign, or post petitions (they really do work!). Create a crowdfunding campaign. Be a problem-solver instead of a problem-complainer.

— **Avoid anger-inducing chemicals and situations.** As a highly sensitive person, you are affected by what you eat, what you listen to, and whom you hang out with. Stimulants like caffeine and sugar can make you feel anxious and irritable. So can intense music, violent movies and games, and places where people are in bad moods. Be discerning and choose a gentle, natural diet (with plenty of organic fruits, vegetables, and nuts). You also have the right to avoid people who consistently bring you down or upset you.

Indigo Power takeaway:

The Indigos teach us to be genuine. No more plastering fake smiles on our faces. We can be authentic in how we feel *and* channel those emotions in positive ways. The evolved Indigos teach us to be problem-solvers instead of problem-complainers.

LESSON 4

SPEAK YOUR TRUTH, NO MATTER WHAT

The Indigo inner truth detector can't be switched off or ignored. Indigos are continuously aware of the energy of truth, and they can detect instantly when the energy wavers into deception. Indigos are the embodiment of truth-seekers and truth-tellers.

So if an Indigo knows about something harmful at work or in the world, they will speak up . . . even if they'll lose their job or their freedom. This is known as "whistle-blowing."

Famous Indigo whistle-blowers include Edward Snowden, who worked for a National Security Agency contractor and uncovered citizen privacy invasion. Snowden realized that whistle-blowing would result in his own prosecution, but he was all the more compelled to come forward with information. Although he lost his job and lives as a fugitive now, in interviews he shows no signs of regret for his whistle-blowing.

A 2015 study of whistle-blowers found that they shared common personality characteristics:[1]

- Feeling that fairness is more important than loyalty to a company
- Having advanced education
- Being extroverted
- Having an internal locus of control (that is, doing what's right according to you, rather than following rules you don't believe in)
- Having a proactive personality (trying to influence, control, and improve your work environment)
- Being a nonconformist

The above characteristics in many ways define the Indigo generation. Indigos always speak the truth, no matter what. The truth to an Indigo is like a lava flow in a volcano, always making its way to the surface. If Indigos hold in the truth, they will erupt in a burst of anger. Better for the truth to be vented continually instead of spewed in one giant explosion.

An Indigo named Shane Lee worked as a manager for Hawaii's largest honey company, until he was fired for creating a public video about the pesticides used in commercial beekeeping. Shane wanted to alert the public to the toxic chemicals that are contained in nonorganic honey. So he filmed himself holding the poisons used to kill intruding beetles in commercial honey hives.

The day after Shane's video was posted, his boss sent him a text firing him. Shane said in a May 2016 interview with *The Sleuth Journal*, "People buy honey for health-conscious reasons. They should not be unknowingly ingesting chemicals which could harm them or the bees."

Shane says he has shifted from being a beekeeper to a "bee-freer" and that his passion for helping bees is his first priority above keeping his job.[2]

The key is for Indigos to learn how to be truth-tellers without harming themselves or others. If you saw the Jim Carrey movie *Liar Liar*, you'll recall the perils of someone who compulsively speaks the truth. Part of becoming an evolved Indigo is learning how to be thoughtful and kind while speaking truthfully.

Indigos disrespect and dislike anyone who's disingenuous. Indigos can feel phoniness in other people, and they won't be phony themselves. Indigos would rather be punished than say something contrary to their feelings.

You can see an example of this in how an early Indigo named Joan of Arc was sentenced to death because she refused to lie during her inquisition. No matter how much her inquisitors tortured or threatened her, Joan bravely told her truth. This infuriated the political and religious leaders of her time, who wanted Joan to recant her story of receiving Divine messages to save France.

As we mentioned previously, Indigos who are unevolved will act in sneaky ways to avoid getting into trouble. At the core, though, this sneaky behavior is because the Indigo is following their own inner truth.

The evolved Indigo will face the situation without running away from it and speak their truth.

Doreen: This was one of the lessons I learned from Charles, who is a truth-teller. He is also very sensitive to energy, so he can feel when he has upset someone with his bluntness. So he evolved to become a very honest person who speaks with kindness, gentleness, and compassion. Charles doesn't blast people with his true opinions, but instead carefully chooses his words and discusses his observations.

For example, after my divorce I started seeing a man who wasn't appropriate for me. He and I were scuba-diving buddies, but we tried to make it something more when our lifestyles were very different.

Charles recognized the toxic nature of this relationship and told me the truth by saying, "When I think of you with him, I feel like crying." That was all he said, and I could sense his emotions in my gut. It wasn't a manipulative ploy, but an owning of his strong feelings.

Since I've learned to trust Charles's truth detector, I got out of the relationship very quickly. I also learned from Charles to trust my first gut feelings with new people. I realized that I had strong gut feelings warning me each time I entered a toxic, dysfunctional relationship (including those with acquaintances and business partners).

This taught me to stop blaming the other person for disappointing me because they weren't living up to my expectations. Instead, I realized that I had disappointed myself by inviting someone into my life who showed signs of incompatibility. I had chosen to ignore those red-flag warnings and enter the relationship anyway. I believed the other person would change or "improve" in the relationship.

When the Indigo Alarm Is Triggered

Charles: Another common social conundrum for Indigos of all ages is those times when in any given situation—be it with family, with friends, or at school—you can sense that there's some dishonesty in a conversation. Maybe someone's telling you a story, and you know that it's absolute nonsense. You know when someone is acting from a place of ego and from a place of superiority. Indigos absolutely cannot stand this energy.

As Indigos, we often find ourselves in scenarios like this, where we know someone's lying to us, and we are at a crossroads: *Do I speak up and speak my truth* [which, most Indigos would agree, is the sometimes-overwhelming urge], *or do I take a more graceful approach to the scenario and just stay silent and resolve to spend less time around dishonest people?*

In a normal scenario, it's generally not a problem to deal with something like this, because in a social situation, if you know that someone triggers your Indigo alarm, then you obviously take steps to make sure that you spend less time around that person and protect those you care about.

In other situations, like at school, in the workplace, and with family, it can be a little bit trickier to deal with, especially if it involves someone who regularly triggers your Indigo alarm.

Some people would just say, "Avoid everyone." They apply a blanket policy and say, "Anyone who sets off your Indigo alarm, anyone who comes across as untrustworthy, as immoral, as a liar—whatever it may be—just don't spend time around them." There are lots of scenarios where a case could be made for that, but you can also get too perfectionistic where no human can live up to your standards.

One thing I definitely regularly and passionately recommend for all Indigos, before they arrive at ultimate judgments and determinations about people, is patience. Make sure that whatever it is you think you feel about someone is something you *consistently* feel about them before you come to any decisions as to whether or not you want them in your life.

The reason why I bring this up is because, all too often, I meet Indigos for whom the source of their feeling of isolation from society is not their inability to make friends—it's not that they're uncharismatic or standoffish. Rather, every time they get close to someone or a group of people, they find something that, for whatever reason, they can't ignore, and it causes the Indigos to not want to be around them. As Indigos, we feel it's so easy to turn our backs on people.

I've met so many Indigos who are frustrated by this. They sometimes wish they could just turn those feelings off and be numb to whatever it is that's setting off their Indigo alarm—so they can just fit in, so they can just be normal, so they can just socialize.

The good news, Indigos, is that there are more than enough ethical, moral, good people out there. If whoever you're around right now is setting off your Indigo alarm, I would definitely consider making some changes. As Indigos, we have a built-in guidance system. It's very easy for us to know when we're in a situation that's right for us because it feels great, and it's extra easy for us to know when we're in a situation that's *not* right because everything in us wants to run away from it.

The unfortunate truth is that we have to deal with the world the way it is today, and we have to sometimes be face-to-face with exactly the type of behavior that sets us up for sadness, disappointment, and upset. On this planet, most people aren't honest with themselves, and a lot aren't honest with each other. They have a warped sense of what is right and what is wrong, and our fractured world is the evidence of that.

In those times, I highly recommend really thinking about the dynamic of it. You know that *you* wouldn't walk around being that dishonest. You know that you're incapable of that. If anything, feel sorry for the people who are acting egotistically. Have compassion for the people who feel that they need to talk and act like they're better than everyone else—for the people who lie, who make promises and can't keep them—because it's all based in insecurity.

You know that if they were happy, they wouldn't be acting that way. Instead of automatically going on the defense and feeling triggered and intimidated by this type of energy, we should realize that this is the exact energy that Indigos are here to conquer, that we're here to shine our light on and dispel.

Doreen: Sometimes it seems easier just to be alone. So the sensitive Indigo may isolate as a way of avoiding conflict. Unfortunately, this can lead to loneliness as well. *Isolation* is when you choose to be alone because you dislike being around others. That's a form of agoraphobia, which is a fear of being outside your house with other people. *Discernment* is healthier, and simply means that you are choosy about where and with whom you spend your time. You don't harbor fantasies about trying to change people. The discerning Indigo simply moves along if they meet someone who is dishonest or untrustworthy.

Indigos and Assertiveness

Indigos who haven't yet learned about assertive communication skills can come across as abrasive, using harsh words at a loud volume. That's because Indigos are so passionate about teaching the truths that they know about.

So they feel that they have to push their opinions onto others in order to be heard.

Doreen: I was reading a social-media post from a woman who was selling her pet dog for one dollar, saying that her family was moving to a new home that wouldn't accept pets. Most of the post comments were sympathetic and helpful, but then a young Indigo woman posted, "Well, you would never accept a rental agreement where your child wasn't welcome and then sell your child for one dollar. So why would you do that to your dog? Your dog trusts and loves you, yet you see the dog as expendable."

The other commenters began attacking the Indigo for speaking her truth, but she refused to back down. Whether you agree or disagree with the Indigo's opinion or the way she stated it, I admire her ability to handle criticism and stick to her truth.

Indigos will always speak their truth. But will other people listen? Or will the bluntness shut down communication? When an Indigo speaks assertively, though, other people *do* listen.

- *Assertiveness* means that you tell the truth in a loving and considerate way. It's a style of communicating that is authentic and from the heart. It allows for two-way conversations, because both people feel respected and heard.

- *Aggressiveness*, in contrast, is where the truth is screamed, shouted, or accompanied by put-downs and curse words. No one can communicate in this harsh context, because the abrasive energy and words make people defensive. No one feels better when they aggressively purge their emotions.

- *Passive-aggressiveness* is when the truth is not directly stated, but is said sarcastically or hinted at. It can also be a form of conflict avoidance. For example, you don't want to do a chore, but you're afraid to say no. So you agree to it but then conveniently "forget" to do it . . . or you perform the chore poorly to ensure you're never asked again.

Here are examples of an Indigo expressing upset feelings in these three ways:

Assertive: *"I feel really upset right now and would like to discuss this with you to find a solution that works for both of us."*
Aggressive: *"You make me so angry!"*
Passive-Aggressive: *"I just love when you do things like that!"* [said sarcastically]

> The main point of assertiveness is to own your feelings in the conversation (that is, start sentences with "I feel . . .") instead of using words that assign blame (such as "You make me feel . . .").

Furthermore, people are more apt to listen to an Indigo if they respect them. Even though the Indigo is accurately describing the truth of a situation, it's tough to take advice from someone who doesn't have their own act together.

The more you can learn to deal with the world as it currently is—while simultaneously working to improve the world—the more that other people will respect and listen to you.

Charles: What took me a long time to learn is that people are a lot smarter and more intuitive about the changes they need to make than many Indigos realize. Since Indigos are quick to make changes, we assume that because other people take longer to do so, they're not as aware. But it's not our job to fix the people around us. We can give advice, but most people aren't looking for life advice. Definitely speak the truth when it comes to mind, but watch the reaction of the other person. We need to remember that every human has flaws (including *us*), and if we focus *only* upon the flaws, we will end up alone.

Use your intuition to speak your mind, and come across as gentle instead of confrontational or critical. Remember that other people have heard you, even if they don't take action based on your advice.

Doreen: If you are a parent or guardian of an Indigo, it's helpful to let your Indigo know that they have been heard. For instance, calmly repeat back or summarize what you heard them say. This defuses the urgency that Indigos have about being truth-tellers.

After all, an Indigo puts truth above everything else. So they *know* they're pushing people away with harsh words and intense, loud energy. But their greater concern is to get their point across.

You can help Indigos temper their intensity and harshness by allowing them to feel heard. Any walls that you put up in response to Indigo harshness will only result in the Indigo getting louder . . . or becoming self-destructive as a "loud" way of getting your attention.

Consider taking an assertiveness class at your local community college or adult learning center; watching my Certified Assertiveness Coach online video course, available through Hay House; or reading my *Assertiveness for Earth Angels* book.

Handling the Truth about the World

The ancient philosophers Pythagoras and Paracelsus both said that our soul is made of the energy of truth and light, and that the search for, and expression of, truth is its overriding drive. Indigos certainly embody this drive for truth, even if it's an upsetting one.

For example, every Indigo knows that governments and other systems are messed up. Indigos know that leaders are lying and driven by ego-based desires for power and money. When there's a news story, they can separate fact from fiction. Indigos sense when the reporting is twisted to manipulate the populace.

Then there are social-media news-feed photos and articles about horrible things being done to people, animals, and the environment. Again, the Indigo sees the deeper truths about these situations.

Yet if the world were a perfect place, there'd be no need for Indigos right now! The group purpose of Indigos is to eradicate corruption and ego-selfishness. Indigos are like the drug-sniffing dogs at airports, except that Indigos can instantly sniff out toxic energy.

What's a sensitive Indigo to do? Well, there are three basic choices:

1. **Detach and deny.** Avoid the news, hide upsetting social-media posts, and unfriend people who post frightening messages. This doesn't work very well if you're an Indigo, who can still sense what's happening in the world.

2. **Channel your upset into activism.** This works well, because (1) it provides a constructive outlet for emotions, and (2) it helps alleviate the problem. Examples of activism include boycotting; creating, posting, and signing petitions; attending rallies and marches; and writing blogs, vlogs, articles, and letters to the editor. See world issues as a Divine assignment, and you'll feel a sense of mission rather than despair.

3. **Get philosophically spiritual.** This means having a belief that the physical world is an unreal illusion in which humans are asleep and dreaming of this realistic dramatic movie. As a spiritually minded person, you pray for situations instead of worrying about them. You proactively send healing love and energy to uplift others.

If the world were a perfect place, there'd be no need for Indigos right now!

Indigo Power takeaway:

The Indigos can be positive role models for speaking the truth and being honest and authentic with ourselves and others.

BE REAL, PRESENT, AND AUTHENTIC IN YOUR RELATIONSHIPS

As we discussed in the last chapter, relationships often hang in a precarious balance for Indigos, who are focused upon seeking and speaking the truth. On the one hand, Indigos have no choice but to say what they're thinking or feeling. But on the other hand, people may not want to hear the truth, *especially* if an Indigo speaks aggressively.

Sometimes the best solution is to create a distance from troublesome relationships. The Indigos have such a strong inner awareness of how the world should be, which is so different from how the world currently is, that it's easy to overwhelm people.

Whether you're related to someone or not, you're not forced to be with that person. Remember that there are countless people in this world (and more being born daily) who think like you do. It's important to seek out like-minded people. Be *picky* about whom you spend time with, instead of being *bossy*. Rather than trying to change people, change whom you choose as your friends. Be aware of what energy you're inviting into your life, so you don't have to constantly struggle to try to change people.

Indigo Love Life

When choosing a romantic partner, Indigos seek compatibility, someone with similar qualities. They also need a partner whom they respect and admire. Indigos are looking for a teammate, somebody who is on the same page and who thinks like they do. They don't have to wonder what the other person is thinking because they understand each other.

Indigos don't do well in drama-filled relationships and can't tolerate being with a dishonest partner. Indigos need to have a best-friend-based romantic partner to relax with.

Indigos do best in partnerships with other Indigos, whom they can meet at places Indigos are attracted to, such as in nature-oriented clubs (hiking, bicycling, and outdoor-adventure groups); in online communities; at spiritual workshops; and at activism rallies.

Sometimes well-meaning friends drag Indigos along to a place they didn't want to go to (such as a bar or loud concert). Be careful about forming a relationship with someone you meet somewhere you don't care for, or you'll find yourself getting dragged there regularly.

Indigos should be extra alert for red flags before committing to a new romantic partner. Notice and don't dismiss any of these signs:

- Bragging about lying, stealing, or being dishonest
- Treating others with disrespect

- Putting down an ex and not taking any personal responsibility for the demise of the relationship
- Abusing drugs or alcohol
- Gossiping, especially with a lot of negative energy
- A history of cheating on partners

There can be a sexual and romantic attraction to "bad boys" or "bad girls," who are edgy and dangerous. It's the allure of danger and having a rule-breaking partner. It's also a challenge to try to get someone to love you who has a hardened heart, which makes you feel special, as the only person who can tame the wild beast.

However, those with an edge often have troubled hearts that are closed to love. They are afraid of emotional intimacy and will push away anyone who tries to get close to them. The edgy lover also has a habit of being promiscuous and verbally abusive. So the initial attraction wears off quickly when your love needs aren't being met, you're being treated horribly, and you're the only one doing the giving in the relationship.

Be careful not to fantasize that the person you're with is different from who they really are. You may fall in love with the person you *want*, rather than the person they *are*. Get to know them first.

Indigo Friendships

Indigos are prone to be lone wolves. They're more comfortable in smaller groups or one-on-one, rather than in large crowds. Indigos look for trustworthy friends who are real and honest, and who accept and love them as they are.

Good friends are honest with each other, but if Indigos find themselves being criticized for everything they do, they will leave the friendship. Indigos are givers, and demand the same quality in their relationships.

Many Indigos start businesses with their friends. Be cautious, however, about idealizing a new friendship. Make sure you have a solid foundation before investing time and money in a venture together.

A "false friendship" is when you are betrayed by someone you thought was your friend. You may wonder why you allowed this person into your life and worry that your inner "truth detector" isn't working.

Don't blame yourself if you feel you made an error and selected the wrong person to befriend, as a lot of people *are* dishonest. Anytime you realize that someone wasn't right for your life, you should *celebrate*, not berate yourself. Celebrate that you got out when you did, that this person can no longer affect you (unless you obsessively think about them), and that you hopefully learned from the experience so it won't be repeated.

How to Handle Family Conflict and Drama

Indigos are more sensitive to the energy of family members than the average person. The Indigo can feel the true communication below the superficial words, because Indigos always know what the person really feels. Fakeness is never tolerated by Indigos, who consider insincerity toxic.

Since a truly authentic person is rare, most Indigos experience family conflict. The Indigo feels overwhelmed with intense reactions to a family member's insincerity. The Indigo may act out by speaking up, isolating, or turning to addictions to dissociate from the situation.

If a family situation ever gets abusive or otherwise dangerous, you'll want to talk to the authorities about it. There are also free support groups online and in person worldwide, such as Alateen.org or Alanon.org if your family members drink alcohol or use drugs, and EmotionsAnonymous.org if you or a family member is experiencing mental health issues.

On Roommates

When an Indigo first moves out of the house, it's usually into a roommate situation to share living expenses. It's super important to take your time in selecting a roommate or only live with friends you know really well. For an Indigo, it's easy to get impulsive and idealistic in the moment and say yes to the first potential housemate who seems nice.

With roommates, clear boundaries are necessary. Before moving in together, decide how you will handle expenses; how to divide groceries and housework fairly; and what your tolerances are for having guests over, playing music, smoking, loud video games, and so forth. By discussing these important issues ahead of time, you can find out if you're compatible enough to live together and avoid unnecessary conflict down the road.

Charles: Indigos are so aware of *bad* signals from other people that when you meet someone who sends out positive signals, you can get impulsive and decide to jump into a relationship, including making the other person your roommate. I've learned to not make long-term commitments with people I don't know. Take things slow, and listen to your gut as much as possible. Don't room with someone just because you share common interests. Do so because you *know* and trust them. Indigos may be better off in a living situation with someone they find boring, because boring energy can introduce civility and peace. Exciting energy often means drama, and Indigos get hooked into rescuing those who have drama.

Dealing with Conflict in Relationships

When you put two honest people in a room together, there's bound to be conflict. They may argue over misunderstandings, differences of opinion, or even power struggles.

There's a big difference between having a spat and fundamental incompatibility. It's best to try to salvage a relationship. But as an Indigo, you shouldn't blame yourself if a relationship isn't working. Not every relationship conflict arises because you're an Indigo or because you grew up in a dysfunctional family.

As we've discussed previously, use your assertiveness when you're angry. Don't spew anger energy, or you'll shut down communication. Filter the anger through your head with the question, *What is the kindest way to speak my truth?*

When the other person is speaking, be present. Drop your defenses, and don't focus on what you'll say next while they're speaking. Look them in the eye and really listen, including reading between the lines of what is being said. For example, they may say that they're angry, but you can sense that inside they're really feeling hurt and want a hug and reassurance from you. Trust your inner signals.

Indigos *know* when they're incompatible with someone. There are clear signs—for instance, if you only get along with each other when you're drinking or drugging. Do you have to twist yourself into a pretzel in order to please the other person? Are you happy sitting in a room together with no television, party, or other distractions? With a healthy relationship, communication occurs without the aid of intoxicants or diversions.

Indigos can tell in their hearts when a relationship isn't working and they don't have time for it. So they will leave the relationship on the day that they have the knowingness of incompatibility and not try to string things along.

Apologies and Forgiveness

If, in the heat of upset, you did or said something that you later regret, you may harbor guilt about your actions. This can lead to feelings of shame, which is a form of self-rejection.

The best way to clear your conscience is to understand the reasons behind your actions. Were you afraid? Did you feel hurt? Did the situation remind you of another painful event from your life? These insights can be gained by sitting quietly and recalling how you felt and what you were thinking in the moment.

While still remaining in a quiet place, send out thoughts of forgiveness toward everyone involved. Don't worry—your forgiveness doesn't mean that you agree with their actions. Forgiveness simply means that you're detoxing your mind and body from negative energy. After all, holding on to anger and resentment only hurts you, not the other person.

It's also important to forgive yourself for what you believe you did or did not do. Have compassion for yourself, and know that you were doing the best you could at the time. If you had more information back then, you might have chosen a different path and outcome.

Here's a prayer that can support you in clearing yourself of old anger energy:

Indigo Emotional Detox Prayer

"Dear Creator, thank You for sending Your healing light into my heart and mind, clearing me of anything negative I've been harboring. Please clear me of toxic energy, and help me to stay focused upon my Divine mission. Thank You for giving me clear warning signs to protect me from toxic relationships or situations."

After you forgive someone energetically, it's time to decide what to do with the relationship. If you care about the person and want the relationship to continue, it's essential to clear the misunderstanding with them.

Ask the other person gently if you can talk about what happened. Let them talk without interruption. If they become abusive, emotionally or physically, you have the right to leave. No one deserves abuse in any form!

Assuming the other person is respectful, allow them to talk and vent their feelings. Don't put yourself down for your actions, though. If you made a mistake, simply learn from it. Don't beat yourself up for it, or think less of yourself. After all, you need your self-esteem in order to enact your life purpose.

Make sure that you have time to discuss your feelings and perspective, too. In a healthy relationship, both people will listen to each other. Tell the other person what you need in the relationship, perhaps with a statement like the following:

- "I have a need for personal time so that I can regroup, recharge, and think. It's not that I am trying to get away from you. It's fulfilling a need that makes me easier to be around."

or

- "I feel loved and cared for when you ask me how my day was and when you share with me about your day."

When you feel tension with another person, it's important to clear the issue so that the relationship stays authentic and healthy. This means summoning the courage to have an honest and respectful conversation, which can be started with a statement of the truth: "I feel there's tension between us, and I'd love to talk about it with you."

Very often, such conversations reveal that a misunderstanding was at the heart of the tension. Sometimes hurt feelings are involved when someone believes their needs weren't being met in the relationship.

Keep talking with the other person until the energy moves from tension to relaxation. You can feel your stomach muscles let go of stress. Your warm loving feelings for the other person return.

Shy Indigos

Shy Indigos are those who are so overwhelmed with their feelings that they isolate from others as a survival method. They retreat to their bedroom, daydream, and otherwise dissociate, including living in a fantasy world.

The Shy Indigo needs to have interactions with other people to gain a grounded education about how to get by in the world.

Shy Indigos are also vulnerable to falling prey to aggressive and manipulative people who take advantage of those who are socially awkward. These charming bullies attract shy people as audience members to prop up their egos. And Shy Indigos who are lonely are unfortunately so desperate for friendships that they will do whatever the aggressive person directs them to.

Shy Indigos are, sadly, used by others, if they're not aware that they're involved in a one-way relationship with them doing all of the giving. A Shy Indigo may even believe he or she is in love with the manipulative person and chase after this individual in a vain attempt to feel loved by someone whose heart is closed.

If you are a Shy Indigo, be extra cautious about entering relationships with people who are loud and aggressive. If your gut feelings sound an alarm, listen to that warning! You have the right to say no to requests for your time and energy, especially if they don't feel right.

Being with the wrong person can drain your time, energy, money, self-esteem, and health, and even get you into legal trouble. Care enough about yourself and your life purpose to only hang around people who are nurturing to your soul.

Balancing Isolation and Discernment

Isolation is when you give up on all people, and Indigos are prone to that because they've endured so much disappointment. Indigos sometimes avoid others because they don't want to be in the position of saying the truth and getting in trouble or into an argument. However, isolation will never benefit an Indigo because humans are social animals who need to be with other people.

Retreats are healthy for Indigos because they're *temporary* isolation. Retreat means spending time by yourself, either at your home or by traveling to a relaxing place. The solitude gives you time for reflection and insights about the patterns in your relationships. You can make decisions without the influence of others when you're on retreat.

You'll know that it's time for a retreat when you feel chronically irritable around other people or are confused about your true feelings. Be sure to take a notepad (paper or electronic) with you, as writing down your insights is a powerful way to discover your core truths.

Ultimately, keep your heart open to meeting the right people. Never give up, because every person has flaws and something they're working on, but there *are* individuals who are trustworthy and honest and open.

Overcoming Loneliness and Hopelessness

Indigos often feel misunderstood by others, which can lead to feelings of loneliness.

Charles: Know that those feelings are normal. Not only do you feel alone and incompatible with others and always in trouble, but sometimes you feel that you're the only person like this—and that you're useless and perhaps you shouldn't have been born.

It's the trap that Indigos get caught in, with a negative environment perpetuating their own negativity. But the way out is when you realize that as an Indigo you have a Divine purpose—and even if you don't know specifically what your purpose is, it gives you hope. There's a reason why God made you the way you are. You are spiritually perfect for your life purpose, which only you can fulfill.

Yes, in this world there are people who are lazy and irresponsible and who take their unhappiness out on everyone around them. We all know that the world could be a better place, but evolved, socially adjusted Indigos actually have the courage to do something about it.

There are ways that you can help the world now. You don't have to wait until you're older or have credentials. You can start a YouTube vlog, write blogs, make social-media posts, sign petitions, join activism rallies, create an eco-friendly Etsy shop, and so forth.

The feeling of accomplishment and creating change can be the answer to all the problems that you think you have with others. Your personal job is not to change the entire world. Change what you think you can, and distance yourself from the rest.

Empathy and Absorbing Other People's Energies

As a highly sensitive Indigo, you are bombarded with sensations from other people's emotions. You also absorb energies like a kitchen sponge soaking up dirty water. You may feel depressed or anxious because other people are feeling that way.

This is especially true when a major world event occurs. Massive fear and grief energy is released around the planet in response to a sudden tragedy. This heavy and intense energy continues as people huddle around their TVs watching ongoing news stories about the event.

An empathetic Indigo can feel this heaviness as if the tragedy were personal. This is where confusion can occur for the Indigo who can't tell the difference between their own feelings and those of someone else. It can feel the same, because heavy feelings are heavy feelings regardless of their origin.

It's the same thing when a depressed friend tells you about his troubles, and then *you* feel depressed. You've empathetically taken on your friend's problems, because you can imagine what it feels like in that situation. And studies show that your body triggers stress hormones when it hears about problems, whether they are your own or someone else's.

That's why it's essential for Indigos to have an effective stress-management program, such as one of these:

— **Gentle yoga.** When you're stressed, you tend to tighten your muscles and your breathing is shallow, which can lead to stress hormones pouring into your body and storage of traumatic memories in your muscles. We can't emphasize enough how important it is to stand up and move around if you're stressed. Any movement is helpful, but gentle yoga is the single best outlet for stress. Research shows that doing gentle yoga for at least 35 minutes a day helps reduce stress hormones. Gentle yoga is slower paced than regular or intermediate yoga, so it's meditative. You can take a gentle yoga class at any yoga studio, hire a yoga instructor to give you private instruction at your home or at the studio, or safely follow along during one of the free YouTube yoga classes. Make sure the class is labeled "Gentle" or "Restorative."

— **Time in nature.** It's essential to move your body whenever you're stressed. The body naturally wants to move, and as mentioned earlier, we believe this is a core reason for "hyperactive" behavior, which is really the body's way of coping with stressful situations (plus, dietary stimulants increase the feelings of stress, anxiety, and hyperness). What better place to move your body than outdoors? When you are in the sunlight, more serotonin—the brain chemical that is artificially stimulated by Ritalin and similar drugs—is naturally created. So ride your bicycle, go for a hike, walk your dog, do yoga at the beach . . . anything that involves gentle movement outdoors.

— **A trustworthy counselor.** Everyone needs a confidant, and maybe you have a best friend in whom you can confide all of your secrets and feelings. Sometimes, though, a professional counselor gives an objective (unbiased) viewpoint. A counselor can help you understand yourself better, which is helpful for gaining self-confidence and self-love. Look for a counselor who specializes in trauma recovery, as this extra training leads to a greater sensitivity to, and understanding of, what Indigos experience.

— **Journaling.** Writing about your emotions helps you realize how you really feel and think about situations and people. A journal focuses upon the inner process within you instead of just describing what happened, like keeping a diary. (And who knows? Your journal may be the basis of your best-selling book!)

— **Calming diet.** If you're prone to anxiety, you'll want to steer your diet in the direction of calming foods and beverages. That means two things:

1. Avoid stimulants, like sugar, caffeine, vinegar, aged cheese, and chocolate (which only give you temporary energy, followed by a crash).

2. Consume calming foods and liquids, like potatoes, brown rice, chamomile tea, apples, mangoes, almonds, and almond milk. Tune in to your body before and after consuming something, and you'll instantly know if your diet needs to be adjusted to support your mood and energy levels.

— **Creative expression.** Sometimes talking about your emotions is an insufficient way of conveying their depths. That's when creativity, like painting, songwriting, photography, dance, poetry, and so forth, is helpful in expressing and releasing your feelings. If you showcase your creative project publicly, you can help others know that they're not alone in their feelings. Creativity also allows you to escape the ordinary world and enter a timeless space without limits.

— **Spirituality.** Believing in a higher power is comforting and stress-relieving. Whether you have traditional or alternative spiritual beliefs, having a loving and trusting connection with your Creator will help you feel less alone in this world.

Indigos know that the most important relationship is the one you have with yourself. An Indigo won't be fake in order to impress people. They're willing to wait until they meet someone who appreciates them for who they are authentically.

Indigo Power takeaway:

Indigos show us how to be real, present, and authentic, seeking out and enjoying healthy, honest relationships.

LIVE AND WORK YOUR TRUTH

Indigos teach us to be authentic in our relationships and also in our work. So many exciting businesses, inventions, and careers are being launched right now by Indigos who refuse to conform or comply!

Technical Indigos

Most Indigos were raised with technology and dream of improving the world through technological advances and online ventures.

One such Indigo is Alexis Ohanian, who at age 22 started the Internet site Reddit as a statement about freedom of speech. His overriding principles are "to make the world suck less, be true to yourself, and speak your mind." When he returned to his high school to give a speech 14 years after delivering his class's commencement address, Alexis was kicked out of his school building when he used raw language.

While still an undergraduate in college, Alexis had the idea to create a website that users could contribute to by voting on and submitting stories. He and his friend Steve Huffman launched Reddit; a little over one year later, it was sold to a major media corporation. Now Alexis spends his time encouraging other young people toward entrepreneurship, particularly in tech environments. He also fights for Internet privacy rights and volunteers for charities.

Alexis is an example of an Indigo who turned his propensity for honesty into a viable business venture.

Very often, Indigos start businesses to solve a problem. For example, a young woman named Jewel Burks worked in the automotive parts industry. As an Indigo, she had little tolerance for the inefficient and cumbersome way in which used parts were identified so that consumers could buy replacements.

So Jewel decided to fix the system! She worked with developers and raised money through venture capitalists. The result is a site called Partpic where consumers can upload photos of the part they are trying to replace. Through image recognition systems, people can now purchase replacement parts much more efficiently. All because Indigos can't tolerate incompetence!

Both Alexis and Jewel share the common Indigo trait of partnering with people who have more technical skills than they do. Instead of trying to change themselves to comply with current societal expectations, Alexis and Jewel capitalized upon their Indigo traits, and the results have been fantastic. Not only are they helping other people, but they are also enjoying the satisfaction of success in business.

Another example is Brian Chesky, co-founder of Airbnb. Brian was living in San Francisco when a conference sold out all nearby hotel rooms. So Brian and his roommates, who were too broke to pay that month's rent, decided to rent out their apartment to conference attendees. Since their apartment had three airbeds, they marketed their new business as "Airbed and Breakfast," and Airbnb was born.

Brian, whose motto is "F#@ Hotels" (how Indigo is that?), channeled his feelings into his online business, which is now valued at more than $20 billion and has helped over 60 million people (including the two of us) find accommodations.

Many popular tech businesses were started by young Indigos who saw possibilities, not limits. They include Facebook, Dropbox, Napster, Google, Spotify, and more.

Indigos Solving Social and Ecological Problems

Indigos are possibility thinkers. They look for solutions instead of being bummed out about the problem. The results are inspiring, such as the nonprofit Kiva, which gives small-business loans to entrepreneurs, often in developing countries.

Kiva was founded by a young woman named Jessica Jackley, who also co-founded the crowdfunding platform ProFounder, allowing entrepreneurs to receive investments from anyone, such as friends, family members, and others in the community.

Doreen: I was introduced to Kiva by my youngest son, Grant, who gifted me seed money to make my first loan. I found a woman who was starting a vegan restaurant, and I lent her the money from Grant plus some of my own. It's not like sponsoring a child, where you get personalized letters from the business you're sponsoring. But I did get repaid as agreed, and soon re-lent the money to another vegan entrepreneur. Kiva has been a pleasant and meaningful experience for me.

Another company is bringing solutions to one of the world's greatest problems—a shortage of clean drinking water. Called Desolenator, the company developed a portable water-purifying system that is solar powered. By accessing crowdfunding through Indiegogo, the founders of Desolenator have been able to bring to market a product that turns dirty water (including seawater) into drinking water. Since it's solar powered, the Desolenator can help in areas that may not have access to electricity.

I also love the story of how the cosmetic company called 100% Pure was founded by Susie Wang when she was still in her 20s. Susie had a patent on an invention to stabilize natural ingredients in cosmetics. As a result, large cosmetic corporations asked her to work with them, which Susie initially accepted. But then one day, as she was formulating an eye cream, one of the chemical ingredients dropped on her lab table. The chemical warped the surface where it had landed! Right then, Susie saw that she wouldn't want that chemical on her own skin.

Susie did research and discovered that the cosmetics industry is largely unregulated. Manufacturers put known carcinogens into lipstick, foundation, eye shadow, and such, without warning consumers! (You can discover how your cosmetic brands rate for health safety by going to the Environmental Working Group website: ewg.org.) She also was horrified by the cruel animal testing conducted by cosmetic manufacturers.

So Susie created her own company, 100% Pure, with a full line of makeup and skin-care products, free of chemicals, genetic modification (GM), pesticides, herbicides, and carcinogens. Her products aren't tested on animals and are packaged in eco-friendly ways, and most ingredients are vegan.

Indigo Activists

As we've been discussing throughout this book, activism is a great outlet for Indigos to express their strong opinions. And Indigo activists are making a huge positive difference in the world! The TED Talks are filled with Indigos passionately teaching about issues and solutions.

Even the youngest of the Indigos are speaking up!

- Xiuhtezcatl Martinez (born 2000) has been giving speeches about environmentalism since age 6. He is now the youth director of the activist organization Earth Guardians.

- Malala Yousafzai (born 1997) has been rallying for the rights of girls to receive an education in Pakistan. She even survived a Taliban assassination attempt and continues to passionately speak on behalf of girls needing education.

- Mohammed Manan Ansari (born 1996) is an activist fighting for the rights of children forced to work in mines in India.

You are never too young to make a positive difference in the world. You don't need money, prestige, or education to be an activist. You just need passion and the courage to speak up.

Indigo Filmmakers

Earlier in this book, we discussed the documentary *Blackfish*, which exposed the cruelty of keeping whales and dolphins in captivity. As a result of this movie, the SeaWorld corporation has announced it will no longer breed orcas in captivity.

Many documentaries are directed and produced by truth-telling, whistle-blowing Indigos who want to bring awareness to issues that are often kept a secret from the public. Documentaries have become their own movie genre, and they often result in huge positive change. After all, the Indigo generation is very visual and learns best by watching a video instead of reading.

> Indigos create and watch documentaries because they are visual learners, rather than those who learn from reading.

For example, in 2004 an Indigo named Morgan Spurlock decided to document himself eating only McDonald's food for one month. The experiment was witnessed on film for his *Super Size Me* documentary, showing his weight balloon and his moods drop.

Brian Wendel's life was changed in 2008 when he read the book *The China Study*, which links major diseases to eating animal products. He decided to make the study into a documentary film, which he named *Forks Over Knives*.

The movie includes interviews with medical doctors about the health benefits of a plant-based diet and the dangers of consuming meat and dairy.

These food documentaries have led to others, including *Cowspiracy*, about the maltreatment of cows and the dangerous effects of their methane gas contribution and water consumption upon the environment; and *Food, Inc.*, which teaches about industrialized food production and factory farming.

The food-documentary genre also crosses over into an ecological and environmental focus, with films such as *More Than Honey*, about the disappearance of honeybees; *What in the World Are They Spraying?* about geo-engineered weather; and *GMO OMG*, about genetically modified food.

Indigos and Outspoken Veganism

A 2014 poll of American youths between 8 and 18 years old by the Vegetarian Resource Group, conducted by Harris Poll, found that 32 percent eat vegetarian meals at least once a week and that 4 percent are vegetarian, including vegans (this number is up from 1 percent in their 2009 poll).[1]

Doreen: When I went vegan in 1996, it was because my inner guidance told me that each time I ate an animal product, I was ingesting the "pain energy" of the animal's suffering during its life and slaughter. At that time, I had little awareness of the plight of factory-farmed animals. I was just following intuitive guidance. I've been a vegan ever since, and I am so happy to see young people being very vocal about veganism on social media and in blogs, vlogs, and documentaries. My generation isn't inclined to "push" our views upon other people. But the Indigo generation has no choice but to always be open about their beliefs, and I think that's healthy. I believe that Indigos are so sensitive to energy that they can feel the suffering of animals more deeply than previous generations.

Indigos who are vegan do seem to be more outspoken about their lifestyle views. For example, professional driver Leilani Münter (born 1974) refuses to drive any race cars that have leather seats. She also insists that her race cars are carbonless and not sponsored by fossil-fuel companies, and she has an image from the documentary *Blackfish* on the side of her car. Instead of being labeled as a diva, as might have happened in the past, Leilani has become a recognized role model for other animal-rights and environmental activists.

Indigos always follow their hearts and beliefs, without questioning whether this path is stable or viable. A very successful restaurant owner named Ravi DeRossi (born 1975) decided to make all of his New York City restaurants completely vegan.

Ravi said in a recent interview, "I don't have to put my morals aside to be a businessman. I don't have to put my ethics aside to do everything I want to do." That is the Indigo motto for work and for life: *Always live your truth.*

Indigo Power takeaway:

Indigos teach us that our work needs to reflect our values. There is no need to compromise your beliefs to earn a paycheck.

LESSON 7

HONOR YOUR SPIRITUAL SENSITIVITY AND GIFTS

In addition to being activists and entrepreneurs, Indigos are master manifesters, healers, and lightworkers.

Healing Energy

Indigos are natural healers once they detox their own energies of negativity and chemicals. Everyone has negative thoughts occasionally, and as long as you manage these thoughts, you can be a very powerful and effective healer. Most Indigos are able to direct their focus and energy to send waves of healing to help people, animals, and the earth.

Indigos do well in taking classes on energy healing to gain confidence and learn practical skills. As they mature with their healing work, Indigos also are good at teaching others how to heal.

Working with Angels

Indigos do very well in working with angels. The intuitive nature of Indigos allows them to feel the angelic connection deeply. Many Indigos are psychic and can easily see, feel, and hear angels. They can even teach their parents and others how to connect with angels!

Guardian Angels

Each person is assigned one or more guardian angels by the Creator God. These are pure loving beings different from deceased loved ones (who can play an angelic role in your life, but technically aren't celestial angels).

You don't need to "earn" having an angel; it's part of everyone's physiology. We believe that people couldn't survive on Earth without their angels' presence.

The angels are inherently nondenominational, meaning that they don't belong to—or require you to belong to—any specific religion. In fact, angels don't require *anything* from you. They aren't judgmental; they are caring and unconditionally loving.

We don't worship angels or pray to them. However, we do recognize that our Creator gave us angels for a reason, so we work with them as God intended.

The angels enact God's will, so they have a vested interest in helping you stay alive, safe, and on the path of your life purpose, as this is God's will for everyone. So angels do their best to guide you in the right direction by giving you gut feelings, repetitive ideas, epiphanies, dreams, and signs. As long as you recognize, trust, and follow these signs, you remain safe and life is harmonious. Ignore the red-flag warnings of the angels, though, and you may wonder how God "allowed" bad things to happen to you.

God and the angels respect your freewill choices. So the angels won't interfere with your decisions even if they aren't the best decisions. If you take a moment to pray or ask for Divine guidance, you will get gut feelings and downloaded thoughts steering you in the better direction.

The nice thing is that it doesn't matter how you ask for God's help, but only that you *do* ask for help. You can think your question or request to God and the angels, and they hear your thoughts. Don't worry: they don't judge your thoughts. You can also write, sing, plead, affirm, scream, or meditate to call upon God and the angels.

Angels aren't like Santa Claus or wish-granting genies, however. They take our requests and purify them to their essence. In other words, they help us in the best way possible. This means that the answer to your prayer may differ from your expectations. Be open to other ways in which problems could be solved.

Angels are pure energy of love, light, and intelligence. They do not have physical bodies, so they are unlimited. You cannot bother your angels, nor can you tire them. Only beings who have egos and physical bodies can get tired. True angels of God have neither egos nor physical bodies, so don't worry about bothering them.

Your guardian angels can help you with anything. There's nothing too small or too big for their assistance. The angels want to help you have peace, because that is God's will for you and us all. When you are at peace, you make a major contribution to world peace.

Archangels

In addition to personal guardian angels that you and everyone have, there are archangels who God created to manage and oversee earthly life. Like the guardian angels, archangels are tireless, egoless beings of light and love.

These are the archangels who are particularly helpful to Indigos and their caretakers:

Michael: His name means "He who is like God," and just like God, Michael is omnipresent (everywhere). He is the angelic equivalent of a superhero who can come to everyone's assistance simultaneously.

Michael knows what your life purpose is, so you can call upon him for direction about the best career that will be meaningful. Michael also provides courage, confidence, and protection. Here are three ways to know that Michael is with you:

- A feeling of warm energy

- Feeling relaxed and safe

- Seeing sparkles of bright blue and purple lights (with no health or eye issues that would lead to lights in the visual field)

Gabriel: This angel's name means "the strength of God." Gabriel is the famous messenger angel from the Bible who delivered the Christmas story Annunciation of the forthcoming birth of baby Jesus to Mother Mary.

Gabriel continues to help human messengers, including Indigos who are guided to teach, write, give speeches, create artistic projects, and enter other careers involving self-expression and communication.

Metatron: One of two archangels whose name has an "-on" suffix instead of an "-el" suffix, Metatron was the prophet Enoch, and he became the first angel on the tree of life in the Sefiroth of the Kabbalah. (The suffix in Metatron's and Sandalphon's names denote that they were both biblical prophets who lived so piously that they ascended into the archangel realm at the end of their physical lives.)

Metatron helps those who are newly on the spiritual path, as well as those who are spiritually gifted in clairvoyance and who are highly sensitive and empathic. You can call upon him to help you keep your spiritual gifts and protect your sensitivity in harsh environments.

Nathaniel: Also known as the archangel of life purpose, Nathaniel's name means "gifts of God." In comparison to the other major archangels you hear so much about, Nathaniel has just recently started to work with humanity in such a big way because we are collectively ready to start living our purpose. And Indigos, here to usher in a peaceful world, have such an important role in the life purpose of all of humanity that Archangel Nathaniel's energy can be instrumental in helping them in every area.

Archangel Nathaniel works with us to get rid of the excuses we harbor about making any important life changes and the fear that would keep us from living up to our highest potential, being on our life path, and connecting with what it is that we intended to experience coming into this lifetime.

Nathaniel looks through us to this deepest part of our energetic being and witnesses the purity of our soul and the divinity of our existence, and brings this energy to the surface to help us access the exact reason why our soul chose to come here.

All you have to do is think the name of one or more of these archangels, and they are right by your side. Again, we don't worship or pray to these angels. However, they are sacred co-workers for your life path and purpose.

The connection Indigos have to angels is unparalleled, and even if they are not open to hearing about these sorts of things, your silent continual prayers will do so much good in helping Indigos resonate with and perpetuate the love of Heaven to help their mission.

Jesus and Indigos

When you read about Jesus in the Gospels, you notice his Indigo-like leadership style. For example, when people were selling animals for sacrifice in the temple during Passover, Jesus protested by turning over the tables where the animals were held. He continually taught truth without regard for the consequences. Even though Jesus was aware that others were upset with his teachings, he continued with his ministry.

After his ascension, Jesus also became one of the most powerful ascended masters. He is here with everyone who calls upon him, including people who pass away and find themselves in a dark and scary place in the afterlife. Jesus helps people of all religions and faiths, because he sees God's Divine light and love within everyone. So, you don't have to belong to a certain denomination to garner Jesus's guidance.

Unfortunately, some organized religions, especially when their ranks include those who don't act with integrity, have inadvertently pushed people away from Jesus. The truth is that Jesus is the ultimate healer of mind and body. Those who develop a pure relationship with him have a bright, glowing light, because they feel safe and loved—which they are!

Calling upon Jesus for a personal relationship, whether you attend church or not, can greatly enhance your happiness and health. Speak to him from your heart, and you will feel his love, hear his trustworthy guidance, and receive his Divine protection.

Absorbing Energies

Indigos are so sensitive that they can feel everyone else's emotions. Sometimes, it's difficult to know if it's your own feelings or someone else's. Indigos also feel bombarded with painfully negative energy whenever a world tragedy occurs. Whether it's shock, anger, or sadness over the event, the Indigo feels it deeply.

Not only do Indigos feel all of these energies, but they also absorb them. That means that they drink in the energy like a sponge. If you're an Indigo, when someone tells you their problems, it feels heavy to your body. When you meet someone who's dishonest, it feels toxic, and so forth.

The key is to be aware that it's not your stuff—it's from other people. Whenever you feel down, use the clearing and shielding methods outlined in the next section of this chapter. You should feel better instantly.

Of course, if you feel depressed for any length of time, it's wise to seek out a counselor for support. A good counselor can also help you understand how your thoughts, your childhood, your lifestyle, and your relationships are influencing your moods.

Clearing and Shielding with the Angels

Because Indigos are so prone to absorbing other people's energies (particularly their negative energies), it's important to manage and maintain your own energy field. This is primarily done through working with the angels, especially Archangel Michael, whose purpose is to reduce and eliminate fear energy.

The signs of needing your energy to be cleared include being . . .

- Accident-prone

- Forgetful

- Spacey

- Prone to addictions (overeating, drinking, shopping, gaming, drugging, and so on)

- Drawn toward dark energy influences (for example, listening to angry music, dressing morbidly, watching violent movies, and playing violent video games)

Other signs:

- Excessive worry, anxiety, or depression

- Frightening dreams

- Sleep disturbances, including feeling fatigued

- Self-destructiveness

These are all signs that fear energy is influencing you. As a highly sensitive Indigo, you sometimes find it tough to know where your own energy ends and someone else's begins. That's why it's best to clear your energy if you have any of the above symptoms.

Clearing

Clearing means that you release the fear energy that you have absorbed. It's like washing dirt from your hands.

To clear your energy, think or say: "Archangel Michael, please clear negativity and fear energy from within and around me."

You will likely notice your body's reactions to this clearing process, including feeling heat because Archangel Michael is nearby and experiencing tingles and shivers as the fear energy is released.

Here are some other ways to clear your energy:

- Taking a warm sea salt bath or swimming in the ocean

- Sage smudging (burning dried sage bundles), spraying sage oil around you, or eating powdered dried sage seasoning with your meals

- Sitting outside in the sunlight, starlight, or moonlight

- Praying directly to God to be released from the grips of fear

- Going on a detox cleanse and staying away from processed food or chemicals

- Spending time in nature

Shielding

Shielding means that you protect yourself from absorbing other energy. It's not done from fear, but from common sense, like wearing a raincoat or carrying an umbrella during a storm.

To shield your energy, think or say: "Archangel Michael, please surround me with your shield of royal purple light so that only love can be sent to or from me."

There are many different ways in which people shield. They may see themselves . . .

- Surrounded in a cocoon of light

- Shielded in a suit of armor

- Encased in a pyramid of light

If you are in a harsh energy setting (such as a place that's crowded or where there are arguments or competition), it's a good idea to reinvoke the shield every 12 hours. Here are some other ways to shield your energy:

- Wearing an amethyst crystal pendant, or a pendant of a saint or an angel, over your heart

- Wearing clothing or accessories that have mirrors on them

- Visualizing holding Archangel Michael's shield of armor to block negativity

- Hanging crystals in your home

This is a process of calling on angels and asking them to surround you or another person with a vibration of their angelic aura.

Manifestation

Charles: Indigos are gifted souls. One of the major gifts of being Indigo that I want to bring into the light right now is the ability to *manifest*—that is, to turn your thoughts into your immediate reality just by maintaining the discipline to keep these thoughts in your mind.

Everyone can manifest, but the high spiritual vibration of Indigos allows them to make changes and attract new situations and solutions to problems more swiftly. Yet a lot don't know this.

Many Indigos use their amazing ability to manifest against themselves by keeping their energy full of negativity. The law of attraction is neutral—meaning it applies equally, whether you are manifesting something good or bad.

As an Indigo, you have to realize that your body is a magnet, and the polarization of your magnetism is based directly in the thoughts you allow to exist within your mind and the energy you allow to exist within your body. If you are feeling nothing but negativity, overwhelmed and consumed with disappointment and constantly focused on what you don't like, the unfortunate truth is that you are using your heightened ability to manifest to bring more of that lower energy into your life.

One of the most amazing things that any Indigo can learn to experience is the true power of their being. When an Indigo can muster the strength and the discipline to break the negative cycles in their life through their thoughts, through the power of their intention, miracles of manifestation are possible.

Heaven did not send the Indigo here with an inquisitive and rebellious nature just so we could deal with the disciplinary consequences that inevitably follow. We were also sent here with a set of tools. We were sent here with heightened abilities in order to bring about the changes that we know need to come to this planet. And we can all tap into this Indigo Power.

The best way to learn the true power of being Indigo is to actually practice putting these principles into action in your own life.

I encourage Indigos and non-Indigos alike to shift their mind-set, to be willing to take a chance and replace their negative thoughts with positive thoughts. If you spend your time being excited about what you wish for, excited about what your body knows is right for you in this world—even if you don't know exactly what you want to do or where you want to be—you have no idea what your life may be like one year, two years, five years from now.

The Indigo Legacy

If we can get past our societal expectations a bit, realize the world is changing and we must evolve with it, we can help usher in the most powerful generation this planet has known. When the Indigos have completed their task and awakened us to the truth—that we as humans were meant to live happy, balanced lives—the work of the angels and Heaven will be ever present in our day-to-day lives, paving the way for lasting peace.

Indigo Power takeaway:

The Indigos teach us that sensitivity is a gift, which includes the blessing of being able to feel the presence of God, Jesus, and the angels. They also highlight the innate spiritual abilities we can *all* activate.

Part II

AWAKENING YOUR INDIGO POWER

Q & A WITH AN INDIGO

In Part II of this book, you'll read a conversation with Charles, who knows about Indigo energy from personal experience. His flow-of-consciousness style is reflective of the Indigo generation speaking authentically from the heart.

The Indigo Mission

Who are the Indigos?

Indigo Children, referred to as the "new children," are actually just one of the many different kinds of new human energy coming into this planet in greater concentrations. Indigo is an energy that has always existed among humanity but is being noticed now more than ever before.

Indigo Children are best known for their personality trait of being very resistant to authority, and very resistant to rules. The truth is that the Indigo Children, while often thought to have "behavioral issues," are spiritual warriors who are here to bring about great change in our modern way of life.

The Indigo Children have come to this planet to metaphorically lift up the rocks so that we can see what's underneath them—to move the curtains aside so that we can see what's really behind them—so the lightworkers of this world can make the necessary changes.

An Indigo cannot have rules blindly imposed upon them. They are driven to dissect, to look into, and to analyze every process, every tradition, every value . . . everything we overlook in everyday society and just complacently accept.

An Indigo's job is to ask, "Why? Why are we doing this? Why do I have to do this? Why do we believe in this? Why is this the tradition?"

While this inquisitive nature can seem unruly, even borderline antisocial, we have to understand that unless we are taking inventory of our way of life, unless we are analyzing every aspect of our existence, we can't see what is working for us and what no longer applies to the modern world.

Are you saying that the time has come to challenge our institutions?

Humanity is an ever-evolving species. We're constantly changing. We're constantly learning and growing and building upon the knowledge of the past. In the last few thousand years, with our enhanced abilities to record history, we've learned more and more from and about every single facet of society and human existence.

I think that regardless of your spiritual beliefs, it's beyond doubt that our world could be better, that changes could definitely be made to help our society resonate more with our evolving desires.

Where do we begin? What do we do? So much of our infrastructure is already firmly in place. So much has been around since before we were born and has become tradition—has become solidified, almost cemented in our mind-sets, in our belief systems. So we go through our everyday life acting as if there's some greater force in control of whether or not we can be happy.

How much are we capable of achieving? What is possible? What is *im*possible on this planet?

More and more people are finding less and less fulfillment. More people are on medication—antidepressants, antipsychotics—now than ever before. A psychologist would tell you that the causes are just chemical imbalances. That, properly diagnosed, they're treatable diseases.

The truth—what we have to come to realize—is that our evolving energy as light beings is no longer compatible with the rigidity of a capitalistic world. That consumerism has lost its hold on us. We're no longer captivated by what we can materially create with our hands.

We're all standing around looking at each other, wondering, *What's next?* We all know that life can be better than this. The change is upon us. It's just a matter of us learning to accept that it's coming, and to embrace and protect the children who are going to bring it.

Are Indigos innately spiritual?

An Indigo Child cannot be subdued spiritually. I'm not saying that all Indigo Children are naturally open to spiritual thoughts, but an Indigo Child does come into this world with a few inherent beliefs:

- Everything should be balanced and transparent.

- Every rule should have an explanation and a definitive meaning that actually applies to the given situation.

- Blanket rules, standards, and limitations are like poison.

An Indigo simply cannot understand why, in our world, we impose so many arbitrary limitations on ourselves. Why do we refuse to be happy? Why do we refuse to have fun? Why does adulthood seem to be synonymous with a rejection of the magic of imagination and possibility?

Indigos represent the new energy that's here to open our eyes to our complacency. They're here to open our eyes to the fact that we've written rules for ourselves—rules that we consider to be responsible and adult and mature but which in actuality are not working for us at all. Are they?

One of my favorite quotes, which I heard from a teacher I used to work with, is "How do we know what we need to work on if it never comes up?" There is such profundity in that question. If we go through our everyday lives just talking about problems at the watercooler, listening to the news describe the things going wrong with this planet, and then sitting around at home wondering what can be done, it's not proactive enough.

You see, Heaven knows this. Heaven knows that our world needs change, that we lack fulfillment in our everyday lives—that even if we have a high-paying job, even if we have a senior position in some corporation, it's only material. It doesn't speak to our *soul*; it very rarely offers the soul fulfillment that our spiritual, energetic selves actually desire.

Are Indigos here to show us our own spiritual deficits, then?

The Indigo Children are here as mirrors. They are here to throw our rules back in our faces. They are here to see through the lies, because one notable quality about Indigo

Children is they have built-in truth detectors. Not only do they know when you are lying to them, but they also know when you are lying to *yourself.* And it's almost impossible to keep an Indigo Child happy if you yourself are denying the unhappiness that exists in your life.

If you think about it, breaking through the complacency should be *rejoiced* (as frustrating as that can be from a parental standpoint). They want us to actually think about our world, not just be born into it, assimilate into it, complain about it when we have an opportunity, but spend the rest of our lives perpetuating it simply because that's "what is done." And it's not to say that every aspect of our modern-day society needs changing, but some parts are outdated; some parts are based in fear.

There are aspects of our world that cause people to believe that the only way they can achieve any sort of happiness or success is to take it from others—whether that be via a competitive, corporate-ladder-climbing mind-set or via outright theft and violence and victimizing other people. So when you've heard an Indigo talk about the things that make them unhappy, how many times have you ever stopped and thought about it?

You see, even if we consider ourselves enlightened caretakers of these new children, it's still all too easy to fall into the programmed tradition of expecting obedience, expecting unquestioning adherence to the rules and the policies we impose upon them, and that they then just go about their daily lives.

What's motivating Indigos' defiance?

You have to understand that an Indigo does not have a desire to upset the people around them. If you really look at their behavioral patterns in school and at home, what they do is not just for the sake of upsetting someone; it's for the sake of helping those who *impose* the rules to *understand* the rules.

What I mean by that is you can't just say to an Indigo, "Because I said so." You can't just say, "Because that's how it is." An Indigo needs to understand matters on a deeper level, because the truth is that there are no limitations in our world. The truth of our world is that we can create whatever reality we collectively desire.

The magnitude of what I just said is lost on most people, but I repeat: *if we all collectively believe in a level of peace, we can have it.* But the thing is, we must first understand *why* our world is the way it is today.

An Indigo Child is not having fun as they're resisting rules—even if they laugh, even if it seems that they're enjoying the reactions of those they're potentially upsetting. An Indigo Child is living in a world they can't understand. They are constantly bombarded by this feeling that people who really have no idea what they're doing—who are just doing the best they can—are trying to force advice upon them.

Since the Indigos are sensitive enough to know that the adults and the caretakers who are imposing and enforcing these rules aren't happy themselves, the Indigos can't take them seriously. They can't respect someone who's not honest with themselves. If you're living a life your soul doesn't believe in, and you're offering advice to an Indigo to help them follow in your footsteps, you're not going to have very much success.

Are Indigos trying to create a new social order?

We have to realize that we've made very impressive progress as a world. Considering that there are no real rules other than the ones we make up and impose on each other, we are living in a time right now when it is safer to be alive than it ever has been. As evidence of that fact, there are more people on this planet than recorded history has ever known.

Although there is a lot this world should be proud of, there's also a lot that we all know no longer works for us. God and the angels have sent the Indigo Children here because of the spiritual awakening that's happening right now.

Whether you believe in working with angels as messengers of Heaven or not, I think that it's undeniable that all over the world, thousands and thousands of people are opening up to the idea that Heaven wants us to be happy. Every day they are waking up to this belief system in droves.

As people begin to take their spiritual path seriously and integrate the principles of working with the Divine into their everyday lives, one of the first things most realize is that they feel an inherent incompatibility with the world around them. When you work with angels, you understand that the world literally can and will be what we all collectively decide. If we want a happy world, all we need to do is ask Heaven to guide us to create that, and we *will* create that.

We also have a duality on this planet. We have a counterforce of people who resist change, who hold on to tradition, who believe that policies put in place hundreds of years ago, by people who cannot have even imagined the way society is right now, still hold true. While there are definitely some enduring values, many of us seem to categorically cling to concepts of the past, whether or not they work for us.

As humans, we so easily become complacent that we often just deal with the world around us—with things we may not be happy about—and hope it will get better. We have to understand that Heaven knows that we deserve, and collectively are *meant*, to experience a much happier world with less competition, less inequality, less judgment . . . and more love, more connection.

Why are the Indigos here? Why now?

The Indigo Children were sent here as spiritual warriors to help us redesign every aspect of our world. Although the most attention seems to center on their academic years, Indigo Children are going to live long, full lives. In that time, every aspect of society that they integrate with will forever be changed.

To answer the question "Why are the Indigos here?" they are here to help open our eyes to the truth of the world around us. If you think about their energy, you'll understand that they're perfectly designed, they're perfectly soul-contracted, to bring the exact change we desire.

What constitutes Indigo energy?

There's so much more to Indigo energy than just the bad behavior they seem to be so infamous for. We have to understand all the other dynamics of a human that go into the Indigo personality description.

See, Indigos are not only resistant to rules; they are also highly sensitive and intuitive. Even though they seem to come across as hardened and tough, an Indigo is actually a very sensitive and delicate being. Oftentimes, a person is so sensitive that they put on a hard exterior in order to protect themselves from that which causes them emotional or spiritual pain.

Are there differences among Indigos?

Young Indigos, being so connected, being so sensitive, do not come into this world with their armor on. They tend to come into this world very optimistically, similar to Crystal energy.

Crystal energy is just like Indigo energy, but Crystal Children tend to not be so resistant to the world around them. They tend to be the quiet ones.

The Indigo Child will be the one talking back, and the Crystal Child will be the one just silently sitting off to the side. It's really easy to tell the difference.

You'll notice, though, that some of the younger Indigo energy takes a little bit more of an intense approach and has a stronger desire to resist rules than some of the older Indigo energy. This is because a lot of people alive right now were born as "Indigo scouts," who contain a heightened level of Indigo energy but aren't necessarily completely Indigo themselves.

What is the continuing role of Indigos as they enter adulthood?

As the Indigos grow older and integrate into society, their unquenchable thirst for truth and transparency will follow them into their new role in civilization. Since we already notice such a huge concentration of Indigo energy in our world today, I don't think it's beyond reason to suppose that a time is going to come when it holds a majority stake in our adult world. (You'll often hear the Indigo energy referred to either generally as *Indigos* or as *Indigo*

Children. When I personally use those terms, I find them interchangeable,because even if Indigo is an adult, I still consider that Indigo Child energy.)

When this rebellious energy meets the complacency of modern-day society, exposing overlooked rules and limitations, changes are going to begin. There are some very notable people in high office who have Indigo energy right now. So optimistically, so avidly are they seeking changes that their popularity ratings are sliding down the charts because they come across as ineffective. But the truth is, they are just ahead of their time. As the Indigos integrate into society, they're going to have the power to *make* the changes.

We shouldn't just think about Indigos from a standpoint of behavioral or academic challenges, because one thing I hear time and time again is that no matter what you do to punish, discipline, or medicate an Indigo, their inherent energy cannot be changed.

You have to understand that Heaven realized what a shock to our system this new Indigo energy would be. Naturally, we would try to quell their fire, quiet them, and chemically straitjacket them and get them to just fall in line—because even though we all want the world to be better, God forbid we actually *do* anything to participate in changing it.

The more you become attuned with Indigo energy, the more you support Indigos to help them get in touch with their sense of purpose, the more you're doing for the world. As the Indigos do their job, they're going to get rid of the outdated, unethical, imbalanced rules and policies of this world. That's why learning about Indigo Power is so important.

War, the division of nations, states, religions . . . it's all on its way out. Indigos believe in unity. Indigos believe that humanity collectively should awaken to the truth that we're all one.

Earlier you mentioned Crystal Children—who are they?

As the Indigos do their job and create a safer world with less fear, we're going to start to experience a new soul energy coming to this planet. We've already begun to see evidence of this energy in the form of the Crystal Children.

Crystal Children, much like the Indigos, are highly intuitive. They're truth detectors, but as I said before, they don't resist the world around them. They merely exist in it. Sometimes they do so in a way that, according to our modern social understanding, fits the diagnostic criteria of autism. Crystal Children tend to talk later in life. They tend to be more observant.

If you have ever actually taken the time to look into their eyes, you've seen the soul wisdom that's there. Crystal Children, clinically described as autistic, are actually very enlightened souls that are, again, ahead of their time. They're souls that are coming here to live in a world that does not require the same social norms that we currently impose on ourselves and each other. Crystal Children are evidence that our world is changing from a place of fear and control to a place of love, understanding, and connection. Verbal communication isn't necessary because we begin to realize on a soul level just how much we could communicate with each other energetically, and we learn to approach our world more peacefully and less forcefully.

Crystal Children are understood to be the inhabitants of the higher-vibrational world the Indigo Children are ushering in.

Indigos are sometimes called "old souls." Why?

Indigo Children have a wisdom about them. When you talk to an Indigo Child, it's almost as if you're talking to someone who could be ten years your elder. It's commonly described as an "old soul" nature. They just *get* things. They can grasp very complex and seemingly adult concepts with ease.

When we compare our level of understanding at the same age, we often realize that they come across as so much more advanced than we were. The reason why is that Indigo energy *is* very old soul energy. They are coming back with a collective purpose not to just be human, not to just go through general human experiences as so many souls are here to do, but almost to make a life sacrifice.

They sacrifice the sense of peace and well-being that often accompanies assimilation—the reassuring feeling of safety that rewards those who just follow the rules, those who just fall in line. An Indigo sacrifices that peace so that they can bring tangible change to a world that needs it.

Would you characterize Indigos as highly evolved?

Indigos are often thought of as the next, more aware step in the evolution of humanity—the strength in humanity that says, "No longer do we just complacently muster a smile and accept adversity. We no longer have heroes; we no longer give our power away to other people. We now have so much energy within ourselves that we can become free thinkers and maintain that role." That's the next step for humanity.

Indigo, you are that next step.

Indigo Spirituality

How can we get in touch with our Divine guidance?

A very powerful tool in helping to find guidance, in order to gain clarity as far as life purpose goes, is to ask the universe for signs. You'd be surprised how effective this can be when you actually try it.

I suggest you just take a moment to close your eyes, take a breath, clear your energy, and ask the universe, ask this energy that is around you, for guidance. Even if you don't believe in this energy, just take a chance and give it a shot.

Just find that place of relaxation. Just find a place of calm where you're not harboring any expectations, any sense of urgency or anxiety, or any hopes of getting the answer you might think you should get . . . just completely let go.

Ask the universe to show you a clear and recognizable sign guiding you toward your next step and your path in this lifetime. After you ask, "Please show me a clear and recognizable sign," just let go. Forget about it. Forget you've just done that. Go on with your life.

And then a sign will appear?

The interesting thing about signs is that when one is meant to relay information, it will. If you're confused about whether or not you're seeing a sign, follow this general rule: *If you feel it's a sign, it's probably a sign.*

Not only can signs contain very specific and guiding synchronistic information, but many also come to us just as a confirmation that we are on the right path. That's what a lot of people need to find more comfort in. We become so focused on where it is we're supposed to be, we lose sight of the "now" and what it is we're supposed to go through in order to be qualified for that next step in our lives.

If a sign doesn't seem to have any other meaning, its message is just that simple. Signs will always at least mean that you are on the right path, that you are being guided. Just "steady as she goes" and stay the course.

When you receive these signs, take a minute to allow yourself to feel grateful, to feel fulfilled by the fact that no matter what it is that you envision for your future, right now could not and should not be any different. You're exactly where you're supposed to be, which is a Divine confirmation that whatever it is that you're working for, whatever it is that you're manifesting in your life, is on its way.

Do Indigos work with the angels to enact God's will for all of us?

Whether or not an Indigo is open to the idea of working with angels, the fact remains that Indigos have many angels that work with *them.* Heaven sent the Indigos to our planet to help them in their job of bringing light to our world.

Think about it. The angels are expending so much effort right now waking people up all around the world to the idea that their life was meant to be happy and fulfilling and that this sense of purpose that every human seeks in the deepest part of themselves is valid.

Not only is it valid, it's attainable. This is the message that people are waking up to all over the world. As people continue to wake up to their purpose, as I mentioned before, we start to realize that our way of life, our spirituality, becomes incompatible with the everyday mind-set of traditional society.

Heaven continues to work with the Indigos to help blaze trails, to help make the necessary changes with their warrior energy. Like the angels, Indigos help protect those they care for.

The Indigos help make positive changes in situations that need balance.

What spiritual support do Indigos need?

I'm commonly asked the question, "What can I do to help my Indigo Child stay open? What can I do to support his [or her] spirituality so that he can access the guidance of the angels around him? So that he can have complete access to his natural intuition and his highest potential of that intuition?"

Every time I'm asked this question, my heart is warmed. Having a parent or guardian who is so enlightened that they would hold that as a concern—that they would be aware of that child's natural ability to connect to the energy around them and want to do whatever they can to make sure it doesn't become shut down, that they don't begin to fear or doubt their ability to connect in such a Divine way—is a blessing.

Generally, just being open yourself, as a caretaker, is enough to help Indigos live in their full spiritual potential. Believe it or not, although my mother was very spiritual, not everything that she said necessarily resonated with me when I was young. It was just part of my general Indigo nature to question everything, even if it's a truth.

I was so happy that she did take the time to teach me, because as I became an adult, as I grew into spirituality on my own discoveries, I remembered everything she told me. I still remember every principle she taught me; to have learned all of that early on has done nothing but serve me and serve as constant confirmations in my life.

Even if your Indigo Child does not seem open to these concepts, I'm not saying to force-feed them, but don't hold back. If they are guided to open up to spirituality in their later years, or at any time, they'll be eternally grateful that you helped instill these very important principles of energy, of higher vibration, into their early lives.

How can we all work with the angels?

Whether you are Indigo or a caretaker of an Indigo, I would like to give you a lesson on working with angels and learning to recognize the truth of the messages they deliver.

When first starting to work with angels, a lot of people experience confusion about what they have to do in order to be "eligible" for this connection. Well, the truth is you have to do absolutely nothing. All humans were naturally built to communicate, naturally born to connect, with the angels around them.

What we *are* asked to do is actually invite angels into our lives, because even though we know that Heaven wants the best for us, our God-given free will grants us the permission to live our lives however we desire.

Aside from rare exceptions, the angels generally do not impose themselves on us or intrude into our lives unless invited. I can't count the number of times people have asked me, "Why don't my angels communicate with me?" I tune in to their energy, and I see their angels standing right beside them, saying, *I am waiting until you ask.* People frequently spend more time wondering why it's not working than actually proactively inviting the angels into their lives.

I highly recommend that all Indigos who are interested in working with these Divine beings take a moment to do so.

> *Take this moment right now to just close your eyes. Just take a breath, be calm, and don't worry about a thing. Ask that any and all of God's angels who are working with you in this lifetime come to be with you.*
>
> *"Angels, please begin working in my life. I ask you to please give me guidance. Please give me messages and signs directing me toward, and keeping me on, my life path so that I can live to my highest potential. Angels, I give you permission and I gratefully ask you to please be a part of every aspect of my everyday life, and so it is."*
>
> *And so it is—when you invite God's angels into your life, they answer and they come into your life.*

Now the next step is just to let go. When you ask the angels into your life, it's very helpful to know that they want to be a part of every aspect of your life, from something as simple as finding a parking spot to seemingly more complex situations, like finding the perfect job, a soul mate, or your life purpose. I highly encourage everyone who is interested in having an interactive and tangible relationship with the angels to communicate with them on a regular basis.

My mother always told me, "Those who write more letters receive more mail." I love that message, because what it tells us is those who are praying more, those who are talking more, those who are incorporating the angels into more aspects of their lives, are the ones that are going to be receiving more messages and have a higher sense of guidance. We can't sit around and wait; we've got to be proactive. The angels are always there, but they are there to connect each of us with our Divine soul purpose.

The angels don't come up with ideas on their own. Rather, they help us with timing, with knowing the right thing to do—the right decisions to make and when to do things—all based on what we chose coming into our bodies or what our souls know we are meant to experience in this lifetime.

Angelic communication is so beneficial for Indigos to incorporate into their everyday life because the sense of companionship, the sense of protection, the guidance, the higher vibration that angels bring, can do nothing but serve the Indigo energy. Indigos aren't actually meant to be upset all the time. Indigos are just meant to speak up when something is wrong. They are meant to speak up when no one else will.

The higher the Indigo's energy, the more guidance received. The greater the sense of guidance and belonging in an Indigo's life, the more centered they will be. The more centered they are, the bigger and more profound difference they will make in this lifetime and in this world.

I highly encourage all Indigos to consider working with angels because, just like with the other suggestions I've made for bringing higher energy into your life, you have nothing to lose by trying.

I hesitate to make promises because everybody's experience in working with angels will be dependent on the way in which they approach it: their consistency, their energy, and how much doubt or optimism they put into their prayers and their manifestations.

When you completely let go—when you completely allow Heaven to come into your life and awaken you to your path and to your purpose and bring you higher energy, and you feel the love and the connection we're meant to feel, not only with Heaven but with everyone around us—nothing is ever the same again.

Indigos, especially, can benefit from this because the higher-vibrational energy of Indigos gives them an advantage in connecting with the higher-vibrational energy of the Heavenly beings around them.

How do the angels communicate, and how can we recognize their messages?

One common question that I receive over and over again is, "How can I differentiate angelic guidance from my own thoughts, from my own fears, from my own ideas, or from my imagination?" It's a very good question. I like when people put thought into their questions. I think a healthy amount of skepticism is an advantage when approaching any new school of thought, because it means that you're not accepting things at face value; you're accepting them because they actually work for you.

A lot of confusion can arise when asking the angels for guidance. It's really important that everyone is aware, when working with angels, of the many different ways the angels communicate.

Clairvoyance

I don't know if this is due to Hollywood or other portrayals of psychic phenomena, but I've noticed that people seem to be more focused on seeing angels than feeling or sensing the angels' presence. *Seeing* appears to be the holy grail of confirmation—the trophy when it comes to interaction with the angels around them.

I can highly respect that, because seeing angels *is* amazing. Seeing their energy is phenomenal, in fact.

But your mind's sense, be it your mind's eye or mind's ear, is something that you should pay attention to when working with angels because your mind can actually pick up a lot of more than your physical senses can. The mind's eye is how we see when we daydream or when we dream.

A really great way to demonstrate the way images and messages can come through your mind's eye is to keep your eyes open but focus on something in the room you're in right now. Stay focused on that.

Don't concentrate too hard on it. Just make sure that your eyes are aimed at something consistently. As you allow your physical eyes to focus on whatever it is that you've spotted in the room, I'm going to ask you to think of a face. I'm going to ask you to think of the image of the last person you had a face-to-face conversation with. . . .

Keep your eyes open. Keep them focused where you're looking right now, but let yourself see the image of the last person you had a face-to-face conversation with. Let that image appear in front of you. Just let the details begin to form. See their face. You can recognize who they are. See any specific features about their looks. Notice if you can see their hair. Let yourself see that.

You may notice that you can do this, but it is very subtle. If you weren't aware that the angels communicate in mind's eye images, it could be really easy to miss.

A lot of Indigo Children are born with the ability to physically see angelic messages or guidance easily and automatically. Even if they go through their adolescent years and forget about it or outright reject it, they will calm down.

I speak from personal experience. That's not necessarily to say that all of them will open back up to spirituality, but if nothing happens to sour them toward it, there's a good chance they may explore it in their own way as they grow older.

Seeing the angels, and seeing their messages and guidance, is only one of several different ways the angels actually communicate. I've noticed that many of the blocks that people feel they have in communicating with angels are not blocks. They're actually preconceived ideas of what communicating with angels should be like that are not being met.

This doesn't mean that anything's wrong; it just means that they expect it to be one way. Unless the communication takes place that way, they don't feel the confidence to believe that the guidance is actually real.

You can understand that if you are one of those people who may not be naturally attuned to *clairvoyance*, meaning "clear seeing." If you perhaps have a different sense, and you're waiting for the angels to show themselves to you, it can create a lot of confusion. It can make you feel as if you're blocked. It's really important that people know that seeing angelic energy is only one way to confirm its presence and validity.

Clairsentience

Besides clairvoyance, one of the most common ways that angels communicate is through our feelings. This equally clear guiding system is called *clairsentience*. Those who are clairsentient can actually *feel* the angels' messages in one of these ways:

- An urge to take action—the angels are guiding or nudging them to get up and do something

- Emotions—something can feel right or wrong and a heart level

- Yes-or-no answers in the form of gut feelings

Clairaudience

Another form of angelic communication, called *clairaudience*, is when you can hear the angels' messages, either with your physical ears or through your mind's "ear."

Always be aware of your mind's ear, as well as your mind's eye. Here's an exercise to demonstrate the way that the mind's ear works:

> *Think of the last conversation that you had. Just allow yourself to remember who that person was, and to hear that person's voice. Recall the tone, the cadence of the conversation, any emotion in their speech. See if you might even be able to pick up anything specific that they're saying.*
>
> *Just let yourself hear that voice. Let it enter your ear and let yourself recognize it. That's called the mind's ear.*

While the angels definitely communicate with people through their physical ears, where actual angelic voices are heard, you may find that your mind's ear is more sensitive to the angels' messages, so always be aware of that.

Claircognizance

Another really important way in which angels communicate with us is through what is called *claircognizance*, or "clear thinking." Through our minds, the angels give us these gifts:

- Knowledge
- Answers
- Ideas
- Inspiration

The irony of claircognizance is that a lot of very brilliant inventors and engineers are extremely in tune with the energy around them, yet they have no idea of their source of ideas. They may think that they're inspired or intelligent, which is also true, but often with claircognizance, it's really difficult to know that you're receiving information from a higher Source, because it just comes into your mind as a knowingness.

Speaking of knowingness, how can we know we're not just making it up?

The best advice I've been able to give people throughout the years on how to actually put this knowledge into practice and begin to recognize angelic messages, distinguishing them from the imagination, fears, or the ego, is this: *Trust the first thing that comes to you*. When you pray for guidance, oftentimes it comes really quickly. It's important to learn to trust that first message that comes through, whatever you see, feel, hear, or know, as the case may be.

The reason why I shared these four different ways in which the angels communicate is because whether you choose to give readings or deliver messages to other people or not, knowing the communication methods can only benefit your everyday life. So many times when we ask the angels for help or messages, they deliver that information, but we may not recognize it because we expect it to come through in other ways.

Working with angels is opening up a new sense, a new ability, something that is naturally built into us; but just like honing any other natural ability we humans have, skillfully communicating with angels requires *practice*.

How can we practice angelic communication?

What I highly encourage people to do is to join groups, either physically—for example, meetings in spiritual bookstores—or online. There are a lot of groups on Facebook whose members actually practice calling on the angels, asking them to give messages, either generally or answering specific questions about life path and life purpose. Just see what comes through.

The real lesson in this is learning to trust the first thing that comes through. It's understandable that you might not be so sure about this at first. The magic in this is to keep asking and to look for consistencies. The way angelic messages work is that they're always consistent. They don't change with time; they don't change to accommodate our fears. The angels will always guide us to our highest potential even if *we* think that we're not capable of it.

Keep track of what comes through. When you ask the angels for help with something—when you ask for clarity or for specific information—take the time to write the answer down. Don't try to remember it; just write down what comes through or record it with your smartphone voice recorder and keep at it.

After some time, go back and review what you've written or what you've recorded and look for consistencies. You'll find that there generally will be common themes in the messages that the angels bring through.

How do we implement our Divine guidance?

As far as actually following the guidance, don't think that just because the angels gave you a message, that's all they have to offer. A lot of people stop at this point. They get a message, and they know that they're supposed to make this change or they're supposed to move to this place or start this business or whatever it may be. Then they spend all of their time in their own heads, thinking, *How can I accomplish this? How can I get this done?* oftentimes forgetting that the same messengers who brought that idea, that inspiration, are still around them. They fail to realize that the angels want to help them accomplish these goals, these manifestations, step by step.

Anytime you start to feel yourself becoming confused or overwhelmed by whatever it is that you're hoping to accomplish, that's when you should be asking the angels to help you:

*"Thank you, angels, for sharing with me. Thank you
for enlightening me as to what it is I'm supposed to do, either
as my next step or as my life purpose. Now, please help guide
me there. Please let me know what to do and when."*

What role do trust and faith play?

I would say that one of the biggest assets anyone can have in working with angels and learning to trust and decipher their guidance is letting go of the fear of making mistakes.

A lot of the reason why I constantly hear reports about how enlightened children are and how easily they can communicate with the angels around them is because children have a personality trait that generally falls away as they grow into adulthood and become more self-aware. That is, they don't care what anyone thinks of them, and they're not afraid of being wrong.

I often liken it to asking a child to set the clock on their VCR, because children know how to tinker with gadgets. Having been a child who was called on multiple times to set the clocks on VCRs, I remember that the only way I knew how to do it was that at any given point, I had pressed every button on that VCR. It wasn't as if I had an inherent in-tune ability or I was born with the knowledge of how to manipulate technology; it's just that I wasn't afraid to make mistakes. Since I had given myself permission to experiment, I discovered what the right steps were.

The same principle applies to children and angelic communication, in that they're not afraid of what people will think of them. They don't have the same hesitation, the same censoring mind-set that adults grow into.

Those for whom angelic communication comes most naturally are those who maintain that childlike optimism that whatever they're trying to do will just work out. Those who aren't afraid to make mistakes, who don't worry whether what they say might be wrong, tend to be the ones people look at and say, "Wow, that came so easily to her. That person is so in tune. She's so gifted."

The truth is, angelic messages are always faster than our imagination, always faster than our thoughts, and always faster than our ego. We do nothing but serve ourselves and serve our purpose by allowing ourselves to just trust what comes through.

It can seem a little strange to be asked to just blindly trust a new energy if you've not done this before. The thing is, I'm not suggesting you ask big questions for help with huge life changes right away. Start small. Start asking the angels to help you with things that maybe you have less attachment with respect to whether or not the messages come through.

What blocks angelic communication?

The biggest block that anyone can ever have in working with angels is doubt that the angels are real or will actually answer them. If you ask the angels, "Please help me with my life. Please help me find purpose," and then right afterward you think, *This is nonsense. This isn't going to work. This is junk*, that doubt becomes your manifestation.

Don't think that the angels only hear your prayer. The angels and Heaven are aware of every aspect of your energy. That's not to say that they're spying on you, but we are energetic beings, so our thoughts, feelings, emotions, and ideas all radiate out from us in an energetic fashion.

You have to ask yourself, *What am I really praying for? What do I really want?* To work with the angels, to learn to communicate with them, you have to set aside any doubts you have, even for a little while. Just put them aside, because those can be a block. To work with angels, you have to want it, so *let* yourself want it.

Don't be afraid to make a mistake, because working with angels is something that you can do silently in your head and in your spare time. No one has to know, so you don't have to worry about judgment. You don't have to worry about feeling foolish, because the angels never let anyone down.

As long as you can let go of your doubt and expectations; let the angels do their job; and look for the consistency in the signs they send you, the messages they bring you, and the guidance you receive—as long as you can trust that the angels know exactly what they're doing—they'll always guide you to do whatever it is you need to do, when you need to do it.

What is Divine timing?

Angels don't always pick up on our sense of urgency. Sometimes, for whatever reason, as humans we can feel like what we're praying for has to happen right away: *I need my life purpose now. I'm tired of waiting. I want this answer now.*

The angels are only going to help us step by step according to the Divine timing, according to what we're ready for. What we need to remember as humans is that of course we want to be connected to our purpose, to the knowledge of what our next step is, but when we get there, wouldn't we also like to be able to *keep* the things we're asking the angels for? That's really important to remember, because we need to make sure that we're ready for whatever our next step is.

That's why, as I've said before, you ask for signs, because when you're working with the angels to manifest things in your life, some of the most comforting messages you can get along the way are the signs that you are on the right path. That is your confirmation that whatever it is you're manifesting is coming to you.

How can we safeguard our spiritual sensitivity?

To help nurture and protect Indigo energy, I highly recommend that all Indigos and all caretakers of Indigos become aware of the principle of energetic shielding.

A lot of parents worry about how they can protect their sensitive Indigo Children and help keep their energy high at school and ensure that when they come home, they don't bring any negativity with them. Shielding yourself and your children is quite effective. I've never met anyone who has tried it and remained skeptical about it.

Indigos, if *you* worry about picking up on lower energy, if you worry about your ability to maintain a higher-vibrational energy in situations that might otherwise trigger you, I encourage you to practice shielding as well.

The process of shielding is very easy. If you are shielding yourself, you simply ask God or Archangel Michael to surround you with a higher-vibrational aura, a light that can deflect whatever lower-vibrational energy you are trying to keep away from you.

However you do this process is fine. There is no wrong way to shield. You don't even have to visualize anything; you can just ask the angels, "Please surround me and shield me from this energy," and they'll know what to do.

Shielding happens according to our free will. Shields will last as long as we feel confident that they are there. The second we start to feel vulnerable, afraid, or affected by lower energy, we then begin to attract more of that lower energy. That is our sign to re-shield. Just ask Archangel Michael or whichever angel you are working with to redo the shield, to once again surround and protect you. The more you do so, the longer the shield lasts and the more effective it feels.

Do you recommend calling upon particular angels?

There are some specific angels who I find indispensable in helping to protect the extremely sensitive and high-vibrational Indigo energy.

Archangel Michael

I am, of course, going to start with Archangel Michael, who has a task very similar to that of Indigos: to help rid the world of fear. Archangel Michael can protect and shield Indigos in two very important ways:

1. With purple light Archangel Michael can protect Indigos from all lower energy, from any judgment. Asking Archangel Michael to surround an Indigo (or anyone) with purple light helps ensure that no lower-vibrational energy can come through to them. Anytime you feel vulnerable to the vibration, essence, or aura of a given situation, person, or group of people, just try calling on Archangel Michael and ask him to surround you and protect you from that vibration, and know that it is done.

2. Archangel Michael also works with white light for physical protection. It does not make anyone invincible, but it helps bring a sense of peace and calm to any situation where there might be a fear of physical danger. Archangel Michael's white light helps ensure that anyone surrounded with it does not experience any more pain than they are Divinely meant to, according to their soul contract.

I would like to say that none of us is ever meant to experience pain, but a lot of us *are* meant to. We are here to be humans, and we need to remember that. Our human experience is also about the fragility of being human and the inevitability of the finite life span we have.

With that said, many people attract a lot more physical injury than they actually were soul-contracted to experience. They attract this through fear energy, through lower negative energy. Using white light helps lift the vibration, helps lift the fear. That's exactly what Archangel Michael's job is. White light helps ensure that our children, or anyone we wish to protect, are as safe as they possibly can be.

Archangel Gabriel

Now with Indigo Children, I feel that Gabriel is a very important angel to work with. Archangel Gabriel's copper- or gold-colored aura contains a very high, uplifting vibration. Anytime you start to feel that there is a drop in the mood or a rise in tension, calling on Archangel Gabriel to shine this gold light is a great way to help bring the energy back up.

Indigos are so sensitive to angelic energy that this is especially effective when working with them. Anytime you are working with an Indigo and you notice that their mood changes for the worse, try calling on Archangel Gabriel. Ask Archangel Gabriel to completely encase them and infuse the entirety of their being, both physically and spiritually, with this gold light to uplift their spirit and reconnect them with the higher vibration of Heaven. Not only does it help those around the Indigo, but it definitely boosts the Indigo's own sense of well-being.

Archangel Nathaniel

Nathaniel is, in my opinion, one of the easiest and most automatic archangels to work with in helping bring life changes and the energy that can be most beneficial to Indigos along their path, both of self-discovery and of self-empowerment. Archangel Nathaniel has an amazing ability to work through anyone who calls on his energy. Like a puppeteer, he pulls the strings to help connect those who work with him to their life purpose. That's not to say, however, that they lose any control over their lives.

It is consistently found that nothing in life seems to bring more fulfillment than living your purpose, and that is why it's so sought after. Living a life of purpose helps you understand why you are alive. It helps you understand even some of the less-than-ideal things that happen in your life, because you become so aware of why you are here on this planet. You understand that other things that happen that seem less than ideal are merely lessons to help strengthen us along our path, to help us help others.

Archangel Nathaniel has a way of looking into the deepest parts of our souls and our hearts—past our walls, fears, and doubts—and getting right to the core of the purest aspect of our existence. The entire premise behind working with angels is that we are all already qualified. Whether we feel that way or not, we *are* qualified because this is the epoch the world has entered. It's a time for purpose.

Indigos are benefited by the easy and fear-relieving nature of working with Archangel Nathaniel. Now, I want to make sure to let you know that Archangel Nathaniel's energy is so effective that if you call on him to help connect you with your life purpose, to help turn the fire of your passions, of your desires, into the reality around you, it *will* happen. But with any change, there is always a transition period.

Be aware that depending on how true to yourself you've been in your life, depending on how many changes may be required in order to get your life attuned to the highest vibration, this transition period can be more or less prolonged. It's unique to each individual.

Archangel Nathaniel has never let anyone down. But obviously, making changes requires eliminating certain things from our lives, and the transition period is merely waiting for the higher-energy replacement to come along.

I've worked with a few people who have called on Nathaniel and were guided to make social changes or job changes, and during the transition period, they felt insecure. They grew a little scared or lonely and wondered if perhaps they had made a mistake. I definitely empathize with these feelings, but not one of those people has failed to receive continuing guidance from Nathaniel until the point where they realized *why* they were meant to make certain changes in their lives.

Now I state this disclaimer not to scare anyone, but because it's the reality of working with Nathaniel. His energy is *so* automatic and easy that we don't even realize we are being guided by an angel. We just have fewer excuses. We have less tolerance for anything that does not help elevate our energy.

Archangel Nathaniel has a very definitive, decisive energy. When working with him, we become equally definitive and decisive. Anything that does not serve our path or our purpose is easily discarded from our lives.

Anytime you feel that the changes are too much or things have become too intense, you can always ask Archangel Nathaniel to please back off. But in all of my experience working with Indigos and Archangel Nathaniel, I have rarely encountered a circumstance in which the changes or the energy were "too much" for the powerful Indigo vibration.

If you are curious about what you should be doing in your life and what changes you could make to help bring yourself more happiness, balance, and peace, I highly encourage you to consider partnering with Archangel Nathaniel on your path.

Calling on Nathaniel is no different from working with any other angel of God. Simply ask him to come to you.

> *We ask Archangel Nathaniel to look into the deepest aspect of ourselves, to look into our hearts, to look past our walls, to look past any of our disguises.*
>
> *We hold our hearts open to this amazing archangel as we ask Nathaniel to see the truth of our soul, the truth of our existence, and reconnect our lives with this energy:*
>
> *"Dear God and Archagel Nathaniel, please guide me to my purpose. Please make me aware of what it is that I am meant to do in this lifetime. Please help bring me a sense of home and belonging, clarity, comfort, peace, and happiness. Archangel Nathaniel, I am ready to live my purpose."*

Besides working with angels, what else can uplift Indigos' energy?

On top of the many benefits that Indigos can experience in establishing a relationship and regular communication with the angels around them, many have found that working with actual crystals can have a profound impact on Indigo energy. Crystals amplify energy in computers, medical devices, and watches through a process called the *piezoelectric effect.*

I'd like to suggest a few crystals that help amplify and balance Indigo energy:

— The first is **blue calcite**. This crystal has a profoundly calming effect on Indigos. Something about its vibration just brings a sense of peace and tranquility.

— One of my personal favorites is **clear quartz**, which aids all aspects of Indigo energy. It helps raise their vibration and also helps them with manifestation. Manifesting calm, peace, belonging, and change is a very important thing to Indigos. Just as clear quartz amplifies the whole spectrum of color, so too does it amplify the range of vibration.

Any Indigos interested in enhancing their ability to create a desired change, either in their surroundings or their lives, can benefit from the presence of clear quartz crystal.

— The next crystal I'd like to talk about is **sugilite**. Now, sugilite has a very interesting quality: it actually helps bring in a higher vibration. Just from touching this crystal, many Indigos have reported that they feel a higher-vibrational energy wash over them, coming from the crystal.

For those who feel guided to work with these amazing stones, you might find that sugilite takes your energy or that of the Indigo you are looking after to the next level that you may desire.

— The last crystal that I'd like to talk about is **black tourmaline**, which helps Indigos ground themselves. The benefit of grounding is allowing yourself to be released from any swell of distracting energy causing you to be less than focused. This crystal is also an effective shield from negativity and electromagnetic fields (EMFs), which Indigos are also highly sensitive to.

A lot of people have found that using grounding crystals helps Indigos . . .

- Increase their attention span
- Stay calmer
- Be more present in any given moment

Indigos have such busy energy that the process of grounding can do nothing but help them with mindfulness.

What are other grounding techniques?

Another form of grounding can be spending time outside, a very simple but often overlooked practice that can really help Indigo Children. Encourage Indigo Children to spend time outdoors, to be in nature. Replacing even an hour of video games or computer or TV time with a walk through the neighborhood or playtime at the park can be a very healing and soothing experience for them and have an amazingly beneficial effect on their energy.

Regardless of what modality you practice or what tools you choose to incorporate into those practices, the important thing, whether you are an Indigo or are working with one, is to realize the benefit of bringing in higher energy, of being confident in your role as a spiritual warrior.

Advice for Indigo Caretakers

What should parents and teachers keep in mind when working with Indigos?

Caretakers are well aware that Indigo Children often bring home whatever energy they are exposed to during the day. They then amplify and begin to reflect back into the household the energy they experience elsewhere. Indigo Children are so highly intuitive that they can pick up on the emotions around them. They can pick up on imbalance even if, for example, their parents are trying to hide the fact that they have been fighting. It's almost impossible for an Indigo Child not to just *know* when that energy is in the air.

Teachers can increase attention span by engaging Indigos—manipulating and changing curriculum to help them understand how it actually applies to their life, why it's interesting, why they *should* pay attention—as opposed to just talking in a monotone.

A consistent theme in the advice you give seems to revolve around transparency—could you explain that?

An Indigo can definitely become much more engaged in curriculum and in their surroundings if they understand why they should be. So instead of getting upset at an Indigo Child, furthering their internalization of disapproval and furthering the damage to their confidence, if we take the time to help the Indigo understand *why* they should be paying attention, then we'll find that the energy the Indigo begins to perpetuate is that much more harmonious. If we exert the effort ourselves to approach them from a more positive and constructive standpoint, as opposed to constantly defaulting to discipline, they will be less inclined to escapism and keep their thoughts focused on the present moment.

Do you think that Indigos should go to special schools?

Throughout the world many believe that the Indigos require special schools and proprietary curriculum designed specifically for their unique needs, curriculum that's perhaps more engaging, with class sizes that are smaller and trained teachers who specialize in working with and being empathetic to the different needs of these new children.

I have mixed feelings when it comes to that because I believe that Indigos are meant to be integrated with society from an early age, and I believe it's their integration with society that's going to help them focus on bringing the change that is actually necessary to help bring more happiness and balance to our world.

What can we do for Indigo Children at home?

What can we do for this energy so that we can help them find more peace, so that we can help them seem happier so that they can get along better?

The thing is, for someone to truly care for an Indigo Child, for someone to truly work with Indigo energy, they have to understand that there is no quick fix. More importantly, there is no subduing the inherent qualities of an Indigo.

Oftentimes when people ask me about Indigo Children, I get the impression that they're looking for that quick fix, that one thing they can do to just bring peace.

You'll always hear me say that my heart goes out to the parents and the caretakers of Indigo Children, because as an Indigo myself, I understand the magnitude of their responsibility as the ones ushering this Indigo energy into our world. It very rarely gives you the breaks and the relief that traditionally we would hope for when working with children.

However, there are many things you can do that have proven quite effective throughout the years to bring a level of peace and tranquility to Indigos. It really starts with taking the time to talk with them. You have to understand that an Indigo's confidence generally comes through their sense of purpose. I have found time and time again that just helping an Indigo understand that they *are* Indigo and *what* Indigos are can bring a sense of peace, because the dynamic of actually being Indigo is not easy.

It's not easy to watch people live lies. It's not easy to watch them pretend they're happy when *we* know that *they* know that they're not. It's not easy to be predisposed, to be preprogrammed, to resist anything—be it a rule, policy, practice, or tradition—that just doesn't apply, that isn't relevant to modern-day society. You'd be surprised how self-reflective Indigos are, how many times they wonder *why* they have such trouble getting along. They wonder *why* they get so upset at things.

They are fully aware of the reaction to what is going on around them. They are not blind to the fact that there are so many people who want to change or correct their behavior. Too often you'll find Indigo Children losing confidence and judging themselves, sometimes going into a form of depression because they feel incompatible with the world around them. We have to understand that there is some truth to their perception of incompatibility.

Indigo energy *is* designed to be incompatible with this world. That's where the power comes from.

If Indigo Children could easily just shut off their need to question and to resist the world around them, then their purpose wouldn't have much effect on this planet. Our society right now is designed for people just to fall in line, to keep our heads down and to not make a ruckus. If Indigo Children could easily be coaxed into that sheeplike mind-set, then what help would they be? How effective would Heaven's effort to send this energy to our planet be?

So you can help an Indigo understand that there is nothing wrong with them, that they are not broken, that they aren't the weird ones, they are the aware ones; you can help an Indigo understand that it is their job to question the rules around them, but also explain to them that society is a game, and we all know it's a game. Our way of life is just a game that we find becomes a lot easier to play if we just go along with the rules. Indigos could well understand that. Indigos will accept that in order to properly integrate with society, there has to be some level of adherence to the policies and the traditions and the standards of modern-day society.

But to help them academically and behaviorally, we find that just helping them understand that we as caretakers understand—helping them to feel at home a little bit, to feel understood—can restore some peace. Not only are they dealing with the fact that they are naturally born to resist the rules around them, but they are also now dealing with the fact that they feel so out of place. Then that energy can become a spiral of negativity.

If an Indigo feels out of place in their own home, and they feel out of place in school, it can sometimes be very difficult to bring them peace. So it's actually a responsibility of the caretakers of Indigo Children to empathize with them. That's why I so enthusiastically share all the information that I have been made aware of, that I have channeled about Indigo Children, because the more we can be aware of their qualities and their purpose, the more we can help them understand this themselves. Not only will we bring more peace to Indigos, but we will also empower them to actually create and bring the change that they came here to make.

Are parents of Indigos just rationalizing bad behavior?

Skeptics of Indigo energy often say that the whole Indigo phenomenon is created and perpetuated by parental energy, since so many of the personality qualities of an Indigo clinically match the definitions of attention deficit disorder (ADD) and attention deficit/hyperactivity disorder (ADHD). A lot of psychologists and counselors think that parents are just optimistically wanting to believe in the existence of Indigo energy because it's a lot easier to accept that your child is special, that your child is gifted—that they're a part of a new evolution—than that there could be something behaviorally wrong. There are even skeptics of this work who say that a belief in Indigo Children can actually be dangerous because it leads to the lack of a diagnosis of what they consider to be treatable disorders.

How could so many children around the world simultaneously all have this medically treatable disease? I don't buy it—the numbers speak for themselves. I don't think most parents buy it either. In fact, sometimes it is research on overmedicating, or medicating or vaccinating children in general, that eventually leads people to the knowledge of Indigos.

Very rarely do you hear teachers interviewed in some of these mainstream discussions about the Indigo phenomenon. I work with teachers, parents, and other caretakers in small and large groups all over the planet, and the truth is that the teachers, who often spend more time with our children than the parents do, overwhelmingly acknowledge that there is something different about the new children. There is something different about the way in which these children approach the world around them. So even though behavioral issues seem to be the focal point whenever Indigos are brought up, we also have to understand that there is so much more that can distinguish an Indigo Child from, say, another child who maybe has a different soul purpose and who might have behavioral issues but not necessarily based in the Indigo traits.

Why do Indigos resist rules and buck the system?

While raising an Indigo is challenging at times, if caretakers (and the Indigos themselves) knew just how special and important these souls are, they might view their behavior slightly differently.

Indigos tend to amplify the energy they are exposed to, and they reflect the world back upon itself. It is very beneficial for an Indigo to be surrounded by love and understanding, and it is also important that the energy they encounter at school be positive. Luckily, many alternative schools have been created around the world as more parents seek out different approaches to working with these children.

It should be known that there is nothing we can ever do to stop an Indigo from questioning, and often rebelling against, the world around them, as this is their Heavenly duty. And while we may not be inclined to characterize the behavior itself as "Heavenly," the ultimate outcome for our planet will be.

What's most important is not for us to all seek out "expert" advice on working with Indigos, as we need to compile this information ourselves. The more we can talk to each other and share what works and what doesn't, the more understanding and compassion there will be for these children.

Oftentimes it is overlooked just how difficult it can be to actually be Indigo. You're born into a world that has seemingly formed without a plan or an ultimate goal; you're here to make changes inside of a society that would rather just look the other way when something is imbalanced or unfair. Sometimes the Indigos feel like they are the only ones who are awake, and they sit in utter disbelief of the trancelike state the world seems to feel comfortable existing in.

Change is often challenging, but thankfully Heaven sent our planet a force that will not lose focus, one that will make it a life goal to bring peace, harmony, balance, fairness, and community into every facet of the globe and the governing bodies that oversee it all.

The more compassion we can give to the Indigos, the more powerful they will be at their job. Once they have ushered in the new era of light, the souls of the Crystal generation will begin coming to this world in magnificent quantities—allowing love and peace to be top priority and showing the rest of us what the next evolution of humans looks like.

Indigos also bring a Divine spiritual light into the world; these souls are very sensitive and, when allowed to express themselves without shame, are capable of channeling powerful and Divinely essential messages from

Heaven to those who will listen. Indigos are programmed from conception with a clear vision of the exact amount of balance and happiness our world should be experiencing, and while they can sometimes seem misguided, we have to understand they are also very sensitive and can lose track if not cared for in a nurturing way.

Some of the most common questions we are asked about working with Indigo Children are, "How can I bring peace to my child?" and "How can I get my child to behave or stay out of trouble?" It should be understood that there is no "cure" for the Indigo spirit, and while our deepest, most heartfelt gratitude (and compassion!) goes out to every caretaker of these children, ultimately the Indigo will never be satisfied until the issues of the world are resolved.

Can teachers and parents do anything to prevent Indigo Children from acting out?

With an Indigo Child, if you can take the time to help them understand the rules that you are imposing upon them and asking them to follow, you'll often notice that the resistance level goes down. If a child is just acting out, behaving badly, for the sake of, say, wanting attention or sheer rebellion, then you'll find that there'll be less reasoning with them. But part of the responsibility of caretakers of Indigos is realizing that we need to take the time to explain things; we need to take the time to be transparent with Indigo Children. We need to understand that no matter what our mouths are telling them, our energy is telling them so much more.

The term *Indigo* is often given a negative connotation in the sense that we associate them most commonly with bad behavior and self-disruptive choices, but there are a lot of Indigos out there who don't act that way. They don't get into trouble. They don't cause their parents and caretakers grief, and I think that we need to get past the stereotype.

What makes Indigos most famous, their more shining personality trait, is to resist rules, so that's what people notice more. But we have to understand that their energy is affected by their surroundings and by the people they surround themselves with. It's really important for the caretakers of Indigos to be aware of the different types of people Indigos are exposed to, and to teach the Indigo about discernment in choosing their companions.

What about peer influences? Why do Indigos get in with the wrong crowd?

We have to understand that Indigos face such resistance that they are often disciplined by their parents, caretakers, and teachers, and since this has an effect on their confidence, oftentimes Indigos can fall in with what we would consider to be the wrong crowd. They may feel that they don't deserve better company than people who might also have behavioral issues, a lot of negativity, and destructive habits.

Lots of Indigos do tend to "hang with the wrong crowd" because they are the only people they can find who aren't questioning their behavior. Ultimately, we have to understand Indigos are also human, and what these fragile souls want, above and beyond questioning rules, is a sense of belonging. Again, if they are not finding that at school or anywhere else, they are going to find comfort wherever they can, and oftentimes that can be with a crowd that has lower energy.

Adolescent and adult Indigos need to be especially aware of who they spend time around, as confidence can be such an issue because of having gone through a child-hood of feeling incompatible with the world around them. Some of their choices can still be less than empowering. When an Indigo actually takes the time to really think about, to really be honest and use their heightened intu-ition about the energy of the people they are spending time around, they can usually find out pretty quickly if it's a crowd or a specific person that really does help bring out the best in them or whether it's someone or a crowd that tends to just help them perpetuate negativity.

Indigos are capable of profound happiness, profound feelings of fulfillment, if they are spending time around that same energy—that is, people who are balanced and true to themselves.

Plenty of Indigos do experience this. Not all Indigos are just hanging out with the bad crowds. There are many different types of life paths for Indigo Children.

What teaching style will reach Indigos?

Getting back to the school question, I do feel that extra special attention should be paid to the traditional curriculum, not only for the benefit of Indigos, but also for the benefit of all students. It's proven time and time again that the more engaging an instructor can be, the more passionate and interested the students generally are. With the stresses of being a teacher and dealing with the public school system, with wage and budget cuts and the behav-ioral issues of children, Indigo and otherwise, it's not hard to understand why a lot of teachers, while still passionate about their jobs, have lost some of their enthusiasm in the way they present the material.

If the caretakers of Indigos start to see the benefit of being more engaging, of being more transparent, of being more empathetic—if they start to understand how that improves not only the behavior but also the general sense of well-being of Indigos—that in itself can become the motivation to change the rote regurgitation of information that so much traditional curriculum has become.

Actually showing passion for what you're teaching is the best way for an Indigo to then perpetuate that energy. If you as a teacher seem bored and uninterested, if you seem unhappy about your job and what you're talking about, how can you ever expect a being like an Indigo, who can sense that within you, to develop their own level of happiness, interest, and passion for the material? You have to understand that since they are truth detectors and perpetuators of energy, they're going to mirror back what they experience.

What about the times when teachers who do teach in a more engaged, interactive fashion still experience resistance from Indigos?

I think that it's important for us all to know that there is no one-size-fits-all quick fix for Indigo energy. No matter what we do or how we act around Indigo energy, it's an inherent soul need they have to resist conformity, to resist institutions, and that's not going to go away.

I wish I could say that there were an easy way to get Indigos to just be peaceful, to just listen and just fall in line, but the truth is that until our entire world wakes up to the changes that it needs to make, the Indigo energy will continue to exist in such a strong concentration.

Since Indigo energy is such busy energy, because it is constantly in motion either through physical or mental outlets, oftentimes parents of Indigos and adult Indigos discover that a general heightened sense of peace and well-being can be found if Indigos have some sort of out-let. This outlet can and undoubtedly will be different for each Indigo, but for me for example, when I was having academic and behavioral issues in school, my mother sent my brother and me to martial arts.

To this day, she still talks about how the positive remarks and the improvement in my grades were never more notable than when I had that physical outlet, when I had something to challenge me, some way to channel the energy. I don't want to call it hyperactivity, like the diagnosable, medically treatable hyperactivity, but there is a level of hyperactive energy in an Indigo Child and in Indigos in general. The more physical and emotional and creative outlets they have, the better. So it would really benefit every Indigo and every caretaker of an Indigo to explore different potential interests, such as music, sports, or other hobbies.

It's very beneficial to keep the Indigo mind and hands busy. So if an Indigo is living a life without a lot of struc-ture—if the parents, for example, are very busy or if it's an adult Indigo and all they have is work and other things that are more based on obligation and less in the pleasure of hobbies—then Indigos and caretakers of Indigos should really be aware of the benefits of incorporating hobbies. This gives the Indigo an opportunity to express their energy in constructive and creative ways.

The Indigo energy needs to be expressed one way or another. So just keep in mind that the more outlets you can offer yourself as an Indigo or to the Indigos you are working with, the happier and calmer the Indigo gener-ally will be.

Could you talk about Indigos,
medication, and chemical sensitivity?

As I mentioned, skeptics of the Indigo phenomenon believe that Indigos are hyperactive, behaviorally challenged, and sometimes chemically imbalanced children given a more positive diagnosis of "Indigo" by optimistic parents and caretakers. Which we, again, know is complete nonsense because this encompasses so many children, how could it be that so many should be medicated?

See, this type of awareness wasn't always so mainstream. Children today are actually quite lucky to have such open awareness of the phenomenon of Indigo Children and the changes that the Indigo is meant to bring into this world.

My own younger years were quite divided. My parents were divorced when I was 2. I spent my entire childhood in shared custody, from age 2 to age 17½.

I think it probably goes without saying that the time I lived with my mother was very spiritually educational. She was very aware of the gifts of the Indigo Children and my intuitive abilities.

My father's side of the family had more of a traditional mind-set. During the years I spent living with them, I was actually sent to a doctor because they believed that I had attention deficit disorder (ADD) and that it was something that could be chemically corrected.

In the diagnosis process, the first doctor actually laughed at them for taking me there. He said, "There's no way he has attention deficit disorder, otherwise he wouldn't have been able to sit still and listen to everything that I've had to say here, which he clearly has."

I still find that pretty fascinating. It should be noted that when an Indigo is interested in a topic, when they're engaged, you're going to find a different set of personality traits come to the surface, as opposed to times when they're just uninspired. We're talking about discovering and analyzing the differences between just general behavioral issues and the special Indigo energy.

There are people who even say that the traditional curriculum isn't challenging enough for Indigo Children. That may or may not be true. I feel that curricula vary so widely, from teacher to teacher and school to school, that it's difficult to confidently express a blanket sentiment like that.

What has been your personal experience with medication?

While I was with my father, his side of the family didn't give up and eventually took me to a counselor, who agreed with them that I had attention deficit disorder. As a result, they decided to put me on Ritalin.

I still remember very clearly the entire experience. I, personally, was a little curious about what it would be like to be on Ritalin because I was so tired of getting in trouble. I was so tired of everyone being mad at me that if I could find a quick and easy fix to that, then I was open to it, because I wasn't aware of any sense of purpose.

I wasn't aware of any sense, other than the fact that I could not resist testing or breaking rules. That's why I think I make a good spokesperson for Indigo energy because, again, as you'll hear me say repeatedly, it's very important that anyone concentrating on the energy of Indigo Children put fair effort into considering what it's like to *be* Indigo. You've really got to consider what it's like to look at the world through the eyes of an Indigo.

Now, while I was on Ritalin, the only thing I remember was just the regimen of needing to take my pill at a certain time every day. I did feel like I got in less trouble when I was on it. However, the actual effects of Ritalin weren't clear to me until about a year later when, for whatever reason, I was taken off it—probably due to my mother's intervention. I don't remember exactly why, just that it did not last long in my system.

Literally the next day after stopping the dosage they were giving to me, I remember waking up in the morning and feeling like I couldn't remember having ever seen the sky so blue. It was as if a fog had been lifted from my spirit, from my soul.

It was at that moment that I think I learned the most about Ritalin in direct contrast, because its onset was so subtle and so slow that it snuck up on me, and I didn't realize the difference. But when I was off of it, when it was leaving my system and I was once again united with the purity of my energy minus the medication, I realized what Ritalin had done to me—that it had literally detracted from my life-force energy.

It had put a veil—a subdued veil of lower energy is, I think, the best way to describe it—over me so that my experience in life had been dulled. It wasn't as if I was behaving better; it was that so much of me had been restrained, so much of my energy had been corralled, that I just wasn't able to be as expressive as my energy naturally wanted to be.

Having had that experience, and having had people talk to me about the overmedication of children with this blanket ADD diagnosis so often applied to kids with behavioral issues, I really like to encourage people to think a little harder before deciding on medication as the answer for getting Indigos to fall in line.

Are Indigos "problem children"?

I had an issue during one interview I was giving where the interviewer asked me, "What can we do about the Indigo problem?" as if the Indigos were a problem for the world to deal with, rather than the other way around. The implication was, *What can we do to get this problem to go away so that we can just go back to our happy complacency?*

I have to admit I was very triggered by that question. I kept my composure, but it was something that I didn't like to hear. It just points to how important it is that more and more people are out there sharing their experience and their knowledge about the Indigo Children. As long as they are considered a problem, then overmedication and overdiscipline are going to continue to be the default solution for the behavioral qualities of these children in trying to get them to conform to the old system. As you've already heard, there are so many other more direct approaches that obviously require more effort on behalf of those working with Indigos, yet *are* effective.

That's what I think we should remember on top of everything. The whole experience of being on Ritalin made me understand why my mother calls these sorts of behavior-modification drugs "chemical straitjackets." You might be able to get a little bit more of a calm-seeming energy out of your child by putting them on this medication, but you are detracting from their life experience.

You are putting them in a fog and numbing their ability to express their energy the way that a soul needs to, just for the sake of what honestly I consider to be a selfish desire for blind obedience.

Should we intervene when Indigos' behavior is putting their future in jeopardy?

Now, I don't want to paint a false picture. It is not my impression that a pursuit of getting these children to be better socially adjusted, to behave better, is so selfish. I do understand that a lot of the actions that Indigos take can also be destructive to their own paths, to their very futures.

A lot of parents I've talked to and worked with over the years have had Indigos who have gotten in trouble or had behavioral issues to the point where it was potentially going to cost them the ability to stay at school or, even worse, get them in legal trouble.

I can definitely understand, from a parental standpoint, how there would be a heightened sense of urgency in wanting to help a child be able to act in a more socially appropriate manner when their future, education, or criminal record is at stake.

Nevertheless, medication is not the answer when you think about the whole dynamic of why Indigos are here in the first place. Consider that, although we're talking about a world that's going to experience some changes, as it is right now there are still aspects of childhood and education that are essential to them being able to support themselves and be self-sustaining adults one day. While some of the behavior of the Indigo can be frightening for the caretakers of Indigos, who have a responsibility to make sure that the children are safe and have the best possible future, in order to keep Indigos safe, out of trouble, and give them the best chance possible for a productive future, we must learn to work with them in a more evolved fashion.

Let Indigos know just how special they are; watch them closely in different situations, and see just how they react to energy. Try explaining the rules to them and remind them that you are on their team, even if sometimes it may seem to the contrary. Be transparent and let them know that the world is doing the best it can, and you as a care-taker are no different. Explain to them the advantages of peace, and let them channel their warrior ways into things that bring them joy. If you are open and honest, they will let down their guard and let you in. With Indigos we (as caretakers) must literally be the love we wish to see in the world.

What is the root of Indigos' anger and dark emotions?

So far we've talked about dealing with many different behavioral aspects of Indigo Children from a caretaking, parental, and teaching standpoint, relating to disciplinary and academic issues. But one common question that con-sistently comes up among the many I receive about Indigo Children is "How do I deal with my *angry* Indigo Child?"

I constantly hear stories about children, male and female, who have worked themselves into a very dark state of emotions, where they are isolating themselves from society. Their outward behavior is sometimes very shock-ing, sometimes bordering on violent, and sometimes actu-ally violent in nature.

Being Indigo myself, I'm very aware of the tendency of Indigo energy to get to that point. It's not something that just happens by default. I don't think a lot of people real-ize this. There's so much complexity in the Indigo mind and psyche not only because they are built-in truth detec-tors, but also because they're human beings.

Adolescents, with changing levels of hormones going through their bodies, are meeting face-to-face with just generally confusing aspects of life as they start to realize that they're not children anymore. These combined forces can often cause withdrawal because, as I mentioned so many times before, the Indigos have one prime directive, and that is to resist that which they do not resonate with— whether it is the world, their family, school, or any aspect of social interaction. You could potentially have a pretty unhappy person on your hands because Indigos feel emotions more strongly than most children.

A lot of the reason that they come here with such intensity—the irony of it—is that their emotions, curiosity, and drive for truth *need* to be unquenchable. It needs to be inextinguishable.

As I've mentioned before, Heaven and the angels know that if they send people here en masse with great warrior energy to show us all of our flaws, to cause us to have to work harder, to cause us to have to think more, that our initial reaction would be to try to stop this, consider this a problem, and think of solutions for this behavioral issue.

Humanity's natural and unconscious drive is to try to get everyone else to assimilate, to come around to one way of thinking, because we find comfort in interacting with each other. Thus, the forces of Indigos needed to be stronger than our greatest efforts, stronger than our medications, stronger than our discipline.

As I've said and I'll keep saying, if humanity could stomp out the Indigo fire, it would do so. It is threatened by change and truth-telling. That's why Indigo Power needs to be stronger than fear and complacency; that's why Indigo Power feels so intense.

What is going on inside Indigos' heads?

The Indigos themselves get to the point where they feel completely convinced that the entire world is against them. They feel that they can't relate to their family. They have trouble making friends.

No part of the civilization outside the front door, no part of the world outside their room, makes any sense to them. They feel victimized for having been born. They feel sad. They feel angry that no matter where they go, they just can't find any level of resonance, any camaraderie.

It can develop into this fight-or-flight type reaction to the world around them. There are times when that can even result in violence. Now, it can be very intimidating for anyone in the presence of an Indigo who's gotten to this point. Keep in mind, as I said, this doesn't just happen by default, but over years and years and years of not being able to find any connection, of not being able to find anybody they resonate with.

Usually it's a result of the Indigos not feeling that they have any sort of outlet, any way to express themselves. Most importantly, they don't feel as if anyone is there to listen or understand. That can be insulting if you as a caretaker have *tried* to be there. You've tried to understand. You've tried to talk. You've tried to reason with your Indigo, and for whatever reason, despite all of your best efforts and all of the best advice that you've received, you still have this unfortunate incident, this unfortunate circumstance on your hands.

Now, we have to really get into the complexity of the Indigo psyche in these scenarios. There are a couple of factors at play. There's, of course, the withdrawal, the levels of the depression. There's, of course, just the general hormonal fluctuations of going through adolescence that cause this sort of spike in intensity and acting-out behavior.

What we need to realize about an Indigo is that it's very difficult to gain, and very easy to lose, their respect. In order to get an Indigo's respect, they need to see something of themselves within you. Obviously, you're not the same people, but they need to see that there's some part of you that gets them. Their behavioral issues are way more complex than what we can handle in just a conversation on the couch or by grounding them or taking away their Internet or cell-phone privileges or anything like that.

So what *is* the best way to deal with Indigo anger?

The way to interact with, help calm, and bring peace to Indigos in this state, is as follows:

- **Staying consistent with however and whoever you are as a parent.** You don't have to change your methods much, but the Indigo needs to see that you own who you are, that you're not changing, that you're not acting in any way that makes it seem as if you don't know what you're doing, because keep in mind how intuitive these Indigos are. Consistency is going to be number one.

- **No yelling, no raising your voice, no violence, no threatening behavior.** Do nothing that can send them further into the spiral of defensive anger energy, because that's really what this is: they're protecting themselves.

As I've mentioned many times before, there's an extra level of responsibility shouldered by those who bring Indigos into this world, knowing that they're in the position to guide them into and through life. Part of that responsibility is that your old punitive tactics aren't going to fly. They aren't going to apply here. It's going to take patience. It's going to take understanding.

What should caretakers do after a flare-up of anger?

If an Indigo, after an eruption or an argument, leaves the situation knowing that the next time they see you, it's going to feel toxic—there's going to be some unforgiveness and tension—then they will want to avoid you. They will not want to deal with that, even though they could be fully aware of what role they played in instigating this scenario and situation. It can then serve to complicate their already withdrawn energy.

I want to mention again, I'm not saying the Indigos deserve to get away with the things that they do. I'm not saying the Indigos deserve special treatment beyond extra compassion.

If you are dealing with any of these anger issues—if you're a counselor, teacher, or parent of Indigo Children—I would like to ask you to just try to experiment with one thing that will seem counterintuitive. It'll seem like favoritism, almost like you're rewarding them for bad behavior, but trust me on this.

Sit that Indigo down and talk to them; look them in the eye and ask them what's wrong. Oftentimes, you may not get an answer; oftentimes, they'll say nothing. They won't want to talk. Nevertheless, you leave the dialogue open if you initiate—and consistently maintain—a process where you don't force them into the situation; rather, you just let them know: "I'm here to talk."

If they don't want to sit down with you, write them a note. If they don't respond to it, no problem. Write notes regularly. Don't bombard them. You'll know. Leave little messages for them. Write them an e-mail. Just let them know that you are there for them. Let them know that you care about their future.

Obviously, if you're still going to be upset about anything they've done or continue to do, that's unavoidable. But if you can help them understand that you are not there to punish them and just arbitrarily enforce rules, but rather to look out for their best interests because you love and care about them, then with consistency you will be able to get through to this Indigo.

Keep in mind that these severe cases of withdrawal, these severe states of anger, don't happen overnight. The solution should not be expected to come about quicker than the onset of the problem. And if the sullenness and isolation continues, do talk to a licensed counselor for support and possible intervention.

Should caretakers just take the blame and accept defeat?

It's no one's fault. If you're a parent or a caretaker of an Indigo and you're experiencing this, I don't want you in any way to think that I'm saying you've done something wrong. There are many different parental and caretaking scenarios, so obviously, I can't know what all of them are.

If you know you've done your best as a caretaker of an Indigo and you've tried to be there as much as possible, then feel peace with that and know that a lot of this is just, as I've mentioned before, the natural state of the Indigo dealing with the intensity of feeling all that's wrong with the world. All the lies, all the mistreatment, all the greed, all the comparison and the vanity—that stuff hurts Indigos.

It's not just you. It's not just the parental role. It's not just what goes on at home or at school or in other social situations. It's a combination of everything.

How can we recognize a cry for help?

When you look at that Indigo, let yourself, even for a moment, feel compassion for how intense it is just for them to be alive. I'm not saying that you should think about Indigo energy being synonymous with suicidal energy, but there are a lot of times that Indigos *do* feel suicidal, to the extent that they allow the patterns to play out in their heads based on everything negative they have seen, the world seems very hopeless to them.

When you're dealing with someone with such an intense feeling and such a huge level of hopelessness, it can be really difficult to get through to them—to help them believe that there is something more positive in this world, something worth fighting for, something in society that's worth trying for. To a lot of Indigos, it does not seem that way and they believe that anyone who says anything different is deluded or lying.

Depression and suicidal ideation need to be taken seriously as the potentially fatal patterns that they present. There are licensed therapists who specialize in Indigos whom you can locate with an Internet search. When I was a teenager, my mother had me work with a therapist who took me to the video arcade during our sessions, and that was a great way for him to reach me. There are lots of therapists who know how to bypass adolescent defenses, and some research on your part can find them.

Society seems pointless to Indigos, and in kind of an ironic spiritual way, they're right. Our way of society right now *is* pointless. What are we working for? Collectively, as humanity, what are our goals?

Indigos know that this planet can be so much better. They know that things can be so much more balanced. Oftentimes they have no idea how they can create this. Again, as I've mentioned before, one of the many advantages of helping Indigos learn about themselves is to show them that just by existing, they're making a difference. As they integrate into society, they'll continue to make even more of a difference.

When dealing with your Indigo Child's anger, or if you're an Indigo feeling bogged down by uncontrollable anger and you just can't stop it, then that's when compassion comes into play, because if you fight fire with fire, you just fan the flames. One of the things that can really help an Indigo is understanding that they are not alone, and that their anger can be channeled into meaningful action that will improve the world.

How can Indigos cultivate mindfulness?

Indigos often have trouble being present in any given moment. An Indigo mind is pretty active, and oftentimes they find themselves thinking about more than one topic at once and giving each seemingly equal attention. As a result, the Indigos are known for having less-than-lengthy attention spans when it comes to any aspects of life.

Unless they are specifically interested, unless they have a specific passion for a topic, Indigos tend to multitask even when something is happening right in front of their faces, someone is explaining something to them, or they are in a conversation. It's not something that can necessarily be helped, but Indigos—and people who work with them— should be aware of this trait because it can adversely affect them not only academically but socially as well.

Generally, people can tell when you are not fully present, and I think we all know that about the conversations and interactions that we've all had. I wouldn't call this a pitfall or a negative trait; it's just that Indigo energy is very busy energy because it has so much work to do. But Indigos themselves should be aware that they can create much more harmonious surroundings and much healthier relationships with those around them if they can understand that a big portion of a conversation and being a good conversationalist is taking the time to listen, to actually pay attention.

I think one of the things that helped me the most was when I heard that there is a big difference between listening and simply waiting for your turn to speak, because oftentimes Indigos do exactly that. They sit there and formulate the next thing that they want to say and only half pay attention to what's being said to them, not allowing themselves to be fully immersed in whatever given situation. So taking the time to actually listen to the people around them and pay attention to the situations they are in requires a concerted effort on the part of the Indigo. It doesn't always come so naturally because of the busyness of their minds.

But if Indigos can exert that energy and effort to being present and a part of whatever scenario they are in, they'll often find that their lives become richer, because their experiences have so much added depth.

What about diet?

Diet is something that Indigos and caretakers of Indigos should be aware of. Indigos, since they are naturally so hyperactive, often find that there are behavioral benefits in not allowing the children to overindulge in sugary or manufactured food items.

It could be really easy to buy little pizza bites, Hot Pockets, or other things at the grocery store that just require microwaving, but when you read the ingredients, you realize that it's just processed food full of genetic modification, preservatives, and different chemicals. Yet we put these unpronounceable things in our body without a second thought.

Because Indigos are more sensitive than the average human soul, they react so much more to the different energy that they consume. This is good and bad; it cuts both ways. This means that if we're feeding our Indigos a lot of really low-energy food such as fast food, we're just keeping their minds cloudy.

I'm not here to preach about diet, but the truth is that almost everything that you get from a drive-through is low-energy food. It's high fat, high sodium, high sugar. It's highly processed. It's artificial, and even if they say it's 100 percent this or 100 percent that, it's still made in a mass-manufacturing environment; it's still cooked on a grill that is contaminated with the ingredients of everything else on the menu.

Fast food is something that really should be eliminated from society. Yes, it's inexpensive, and a lot of people say that it tastes great, and it's really easy to just go through a drive-through, as opposed to buying food at a grocery store or getting your pots and pans out to prepare a meal. However, the energy of fast food is having an adverse effect on society in general. Its low nutritional value is keeping us from reaching our potential for higher-vibrational energy that we should be accessing on a daily basis.

Indigos are especially susceptible to the low-energy impact of high-fat, high-sugar, and highly processed foods. Also, genetically modified foods (GMOs) containing the chemical glyphosate (sprayed as Roundup brand pesticide/herbicide) has been linked to increased autism, allergies, and other illnesses.

I know that this can sound a little overwhelming, especially to parents and caretakers who may not feel that they have the time to prepare healthier meals. Maybe they just send their children to school with money to go to the nearest fast-food place and buy themselves lunch, or to eat whatever is served in the cafeteria.

If we want to see a very profound increase in Indigos' general sense of well-being, though, the first thing we've got to do is eliminate unhealthy foods from the diet. Because these children are such amplifiers of the energy they're exposed to, unmodified foods without pesticides are the best choice.

My mother switched my brother Grant and me to an all-organic diet when we were teenagers, and within a week we both felt calmer. My mother still talks about how much more peaceful we became when she got us off foods containing pesticides, herbicides, and preservatives. It was tougher back then to find organic foods, but she managed to do so even though we didn't have much money at the time. Now it's really easy to find and afford organics, or grow your own with the help of your Indigo for a bonding experience.

Is vegetarianism the answer?

We do have to be aware of certain specific dietary choices that may not suit Indigo energy. I'm the last person who would ever say that everyone needs to be vegetarian, but I highly encourage all caretakers of Indigos, and Indigos themselves, to be open to experimenting with your diet. Allow yourself to spend a week or two abstaining from meats that are processed in high-stress environments.

Whether we realize it or not, we take on the stress and the fear of the animals we consume because the chemical reaction is in their bloodstream—the stress hormones remain in those meats. Our body absorbs those chemicals, and it can bring that stress and fear energy into our being. So farm-raised, cage-free, hormone-free meats are definitely what should be sought for sensitive Indigo energy.

A processed diet is very new to humanity. For thousands of years, we ate straight from the land, and obviously in a less urbanized society, it was easier to do so. But the processing and the mass production of all of our food has only really come about in the last 5,000 years, and we're not compatible with it.

Unfortunately, this means that consumption of soda with refined sugar, alcohol, tobacco, and narcotics is going to have a highly deleterious effect because Indigo energy is a magnifier.

Everyone should be aware of what they're putting in their bodies, but this especially pertains to Indigos since they're so sensitive and react so harshly to anything harmful. We need to take responsibility for ensuring that whatever we're allowing them—or whatever we, as Indigos, are allowing ourselves—to consume is of the highest vibration.

The important thing is that you're aware, because more than anything, being observant is the best quality any caretaker of an Indigo can have—and it's the best quality any *Indigo* can have. Just observe what is affecting your energy.

Try eating very healthfully. Try eating organic. Try eating chemical-free for two weeks. If I'm not right, then go back to your old habits. But I can almost guarantee that you're going to notice a difference not only in your own energy, but also in the Indigo energy around you.

Advice for Indigos

What words of wisdom would you like to share with other Indigos?

As an Indigo, regardless of your age, I think what's really important for you to know is that despite how much caretakers, teachers, and others may resist your energy and might discipline you for acting the way you do, you are not "wrong." There's nothing wrong with you. What's really important for all of us Indigos to realize is that our job is unique; never before has so much Indigo energy been brought into this world to create change of such magnitude.

Not only are we not wrong, but we're also not alone. We all go through the struggles of dealing with the lies in this world and being so sensitive to everything going on around us that we feel like the only way to turn that off is to distract ourselves with sometimes-negative behavior or consume things that numb our energy, like alcohol or drugs.

It's essential for all of us Indigos to realize the collective purpose that we have, and it can be difficult to answer questions like, *How can I make a difference? How can I use my energy for the greater good when I'm struggling to deal with the lies in this world and everything that's going on around me, and feeling like the only way to turn off my sensitivity is to distract myself with negative behavior or consume things that numb my energy, like alcohol or drugs?*

The truth is that the way that you can make a difference is just *be yourself.*

Your naturally inquisitive and rebellious ways are forcing the people around you to pay more attention to how they interact, to the very specific dynamics of the world around *them.* Even though it may not feel as if we're bringing any level of positivity to the world, the fact is that we're already opening eyes.

As an Indigo, if you knew how many teachers—meaning people who went to traditional schools to learn how to traditionally be an educator in a public or private school—come to me who may not have any other spiritual beliefs but are so aware and so convinced of the Indigo phenomenon, it should serve to help you understand that you are a part of something special.

You are a part of a big change, and your very existence—just passively *existing*—is already making a difference, because just by being yourself, you are also waking people up to the synchronistic aspects of spirituality that coincide with your existence. You're waking people up to the fact that the world is changing.

I watched a traditional media report on Indigo Children, and even the reporters, even the journalists involved in this report, were asking questions about the Indigos bringing change into the world. The fact that your presence alone is causing people in mainstream belief systems to at least conceptualize—to even for a second think about—the fact that positive change is coming to the world is evidence that eyes are being opened.

If you can't see the beauty in that, then go back and reread the last several paragraphs. Because just by existing, you're opening people's eyes to the fact that positive change is coming to this world.

How can we change the world?

Our world, the energy of our world, is the culmination of the way that each of us acts, the way that each of us reacts to each other and to the existing dynamics of our society. The way, the *only* way, to bring peace, to bring change, to bring empowerment into our world, is to help people realize that it's *already* changing around them, to empower them to step up and be a part of something that already has momentum. Because I think the biggest resistance that people have to bringing change and to being a part of change in this world is they don't want to be the only ones. They don't want to be the minority and begin a fight that won't have any momentum and will just sputter out.

Indigos absolutely cannot ignore what they feel is wrong in this world. You as an Indigo should know that your inability to ignore the problems can seem frustrating.

When your time comes to create change, you'll know. You'll know because that Indigo energy will always exist within you, even if you forget about it, even if you go to school or get a job and just integrate with society and start your lives, and you don't even think about the spiritual aspects of who you are on the inside, why you came to this planet. And even if you forget about it for a short time, you can never completely shut it off because it's what your soul chose to experience coming into this body. When your time comes to make change, you're going to be there.

You're going to be ready. You're not going to require any convincing. You're not going to worry about what you might have to sacrifice for the greater good. You're going to know exactly what you need to do. Whether that's helping to make a corporation more ethical by raising awareness of the problems of modified and processed foods or whether you are helping people with relationships.

Whether you're helping other Indigo Children or other troubled children understand the truth about themselves and about the way the world is changing, whatever it is that you decide to do, whatever difference you decide to make, the advantage of being Indigo is that you are always ready. You're always on.

Since your existence, your childhood, everything about you is already being noticed on such big levels, you should take pride. You should be proud even of things you think you shouldn't be proud of. Know that within the short amount of time there has been such a big influx of Indigos on this planet, already dramatic changes have been made, and they will continue to be made the more Indigos find empowerment through self-awareness.

Are Indigos socially maladjusted?

As an Indigo, it's very easy and normal to fall into the belief that we're incompatible with the general society, that we're somehow outsiders or black sheep. We might even have been called that at times because our energy is so different. Because why *is* it that we always have to be so resistant? Why is it that we always have to be so *passionate* about things when everyone else can just fall in line?

Hopefully, over the course of this book, you have been learning to embrace those differences, celebrate them, and understand how important and Divine they are; and you can actually allow those differences to empower you. You are different, whether you realize you chose this path or not. Whether you feel like you would change that right now if you could, this is your life.

This is your path, and it's going to be a beautiful life and a beautiful path if you can just learn to accept and embrace that you're always going to be sensitive. You're always going to know the truth in a given situation. You're always going to want what is fair, what is equitable, and there may be times where you find that creates what you consider to be terminal social incompatibilities.

There may be times where you might find yourself incompatible with co-workers or jobs. You might wonder why you can't keep a job or why you can't maintain stability because you're constantly aware of the imbalance in any given situation.

You wonder what you can do to find more peace because, again, as any Indigo knows, it's not easy.

On a day-to-day, moment-to-moment level, how can Indigos cultivate a sense of well-being and peace?

As much as you hear people like me talk about how amazing Indigos are and what a blessing to this world it is that so much Indigo energy has come, what can we as Indigos do to find peace? Yes, we're working on the world of tomorrow, directly and indirectly waking people up to the changes that are necessary on this planet, but what can we do to enjoy our life, to have a sense of fulfillment, to have a sense of well-being?

It's a question that I get a lot. It's a question that I had to figure out the answer to for myself. The good news is there is a lot that we as Indigos can do for ourselves. On top of putting a concerted effort into allowing ourselves— giving ourselves *permission*—to feel empowered, to feel special, knowing the fact that we have such a Divine and Heavenly calling to bring change to this world, there are lots of other things that we can do to bring peace and harmony into our lives.

Even if my suggestions don't seem to resonate with your particular interests, I encourage you to at least stay open to them because they didn't come from nowhere. These are a compilation of what Indigos have been using to find peace and well-being for years and years and years. Now that you've realized that you have so much in common with other Indigos, don't limit yourself by thinking that you don't have *these* things in common.

Meditation

Meditation is something I highly recommend for all Indigos regardless of age. *Meditation* is kind of a loaded word because generally it seems synonymous with Eastern religion, with yoga or things that you may not even have any interest in. Meditation generally elicits a picture of someone sitting with perfect posture, their fingers touching together in *mudras*, and all the ritual and everything that goes along with it. I'm definitely not denouncing or trying to criticize that type of meditation, but we should understand that meditation is not limited to just those stereotypical pictures and ideas we may have been exposed to.

Meditation is, at its most basic element, a process of giving ourselves permission to be completely in a moment. What I mean by that is our thoughts are so non-stop—our sense of wonder, our emotions as Indigos are so heightened—that it can sometimes even be abusive to ourselves to not give ourselves temporary reprieve from the intensity.

Meditation is a moment where we give ourselves permission to be free of our worries, to be free of our concerns, to be free of any lower energy—any guilt, any fear, any doubt—whatever it may be that might be dragging us down spiritually or emotionally.

Meditation is the process of deciding that maybe for just a moment we choose to be free. We choose to be light, and what I mean by light is we choose to release the heaviness of whatever might be bothering us, whatever our long-term or short-term concerns may be. I highly suggest that all Indigos, no matter how much Indigo energy you feel you have in you, create and maintain a regular regimen of meditating, of centering your energy, of using the power of your breath to breathe out whatever is stressing you.

This is something that you can do anytime. You don't have to worry about how you look. You don't have to worry about what you're thinking about when you're doing this. All you have to do is just take a moment.

It could be in the shower. It could be right before you fall asleep. It can be just between tasks, where you just lie down on the floor or sit in a comfortable chair, close your eyes, and take a deep breath in. Any worries that you have, anything that races through your mind when you start this process, just passively give yourself permission to release this energy, release any intensity, any emotion through each exhale.

It may take some practice. It may take some time and some discipline to really feel like you're getting to the point where you're actually releasing something when you sit and do this process. Regardless of age, all Indigos can benefit from taking this energetic time-out to just breathe.

For those of you who are caretakers, you can't force this on an Indigo. You have to present it to them in such a way that they want to be a part of it. You have to inspire it in them.

That's why I'm trying to inspire all Indigos: because it's not just something to do for ritual's sake; it's something that can and will bring a higher sense of well-being to your energy. You *will* experience its benefits. Even if you start off doing it just because of my suggestion, there will come a time, if you maintain this practice, that you will feel the need to regularly incorporate this into your routine.

It can really help to put on melodic soft music, generally without lyrics, nothing too harsh. It doesn't have to be classical, meditation, or mantra music. It could be something instrumental, something that you find soothing. Just breathe and release whatever's stressing you, whatever's going on in your mind, and maintain it as long as you can. Like I've said, even if it's just a moment, that will help. But if it can be more, that's better. Integrate this into your routine and you will understand why I suggest it.

Affirmations

To help you maintain this level of self-acceptance in any given social situation, I highly suggest that all Indigos incorporate positive affirmations into their daily routine. Meditation definitely helps calm our energy, helps us to be more focused and more centered and more in the moment.

Positive affirmations are an opportunity for Indigos of all ages to use the busyness of our minds for our own benefit.

I myself require little convincing as to the power of positive affirmations. Some of my earliest memories are of listening to my mother, Doreen—who at the time was a single mom without a higher education doing the best she could with two children, working as a secretary at an insurance office—practice affirmations.

I remember being two, three years old, and as she was getting ready, doing her makeup and her hair, she would be listening to cassette recordings of her own voice saying very surprising things like, *I am a published author. I am a speaker, and people listen to me. I travel the world and help bring light and happiness to anyone who will listen.* At the time, all of those positive affirmations seemed logically preposterous.

But positive affirmations can be especially helpful to Indigos who are so sensitive to the energy that they allow themselves to be exposed to. The more positivity we give ourselves permission to experience, the greater our general sense of well-being and, therefore, the more we crave higher energy, because we start to experience and realize the benefits of it.

Positive affirmations do not have to be a complicated, ritualized process. It basically is maintaining the discipline to replace one negative or fearful thought with its opposite at least once a day. Meaning, if you're afraid that you might not find a good job, or if you're upset that you don't like your current job, replace at least one of those intruding thoughts with a positive affirmation: *I deserve the perfect job. I deserve happiness.* You can modify what I just said to relate to any situation.

Indigos, because of our heightened sensitivity, because of our heightened intuition, have an extra responsibility to maintain a higher energy within ourselves. It is how we will find peace. It is how we will find happiness.

We can't spend so much of our time being upset and angry at the world, because the changes that we're going to make in the world, we'll be guided to. That part will answer itself. That's part of the gift of being Indigo, that our purpose will meet us along our path.

The best we can do for ourselves is find as much peace and tranquility in this world as possible.

By using positive affirmations and making ourselves maintain a regular routine of bringing positive energy into our thoughts, of allowing ourselves even for a moment to believe that we have the potential, that we deserve a happy future, that we deserve the things that we're manifesting, that we desire, we then begin to use the power of energy to attract these things.

The amazing thing about tapping into the power of our own Indigo energy is that we start to see undeniable evidence of just how powerful we are. You'll always hear people talk about how powerful Indigos are. There's no better way to actually experience, to actually see proof of this, than to truly empower yourself as an Indigo.

Try this—again, you have nothing to lose. At least once a day—more often is definitely preferred—make yourself think a positive thought. Believe that something that you wish to have in your life already exists and is on its way to you.

Change your thought patterns. Change the way you look at the world . . . and watch the way that the world changes around you. This isn't just generic uplifting advice for the sake of making you feel good. This will make a tangible, real, and noticeable difference in your life as you start to realize just how powerful you are.

You will start to realize just how much control you have over the life that you experience.

Exercise

Now we're going to talk about exercise. I know this is probably the point where you're thinking, *I've heard enough for today—I think I'll skip this*, but bear with me.

Some people naturally are open to the idea of exercise. Not all Indigos are going to be resistant to it. For those who *are* resistant, as difficult as it can be to hear, physical activity of some sort is a necessary physical outlet.

It does not have to be traditional exercise. It doesn't have to be at the gym. I personally cannot stand being inside a gym. I need the outdoors. I like to hike in nature and run and jump on rocks and things like that. That's exercise to me. I always have to make sure that my surroundings allow for that sort of outlet.

One way or another, I highly encourage all Indigos— especially those of you who are hiding from the world, those of you who are spending more time on the Web than in face-to-face situations—to incorporate some level of physical activity into your daily regimen.

Understand that this isn't weight loss. This isn't "fitness." What this is, is giving ourselves an opportunity to release the intense, high-vibrational energy constantly running through us.

When you have a physical outlet, when you can regularly step outside your door and run, play a sport or just a game of Frisbee at the park, walk your dog—whatever it may be, do *something*—you will find that your mind will be much easier to live with because you've allowed your-self to burn off energy. I know this may sound less than effective to you, but you've got to trust me on this.

The more physical activity you can incorporate into your everyday routine, the better you're going to feel. Probably the most important thing for an Indigo to be focused on in their everyday life is a general sense of well-being.

How can Indigos move into more positive emotions?

Indigos need higher energy. That doesn't always have to mean in a spiritual sense; you've got to look at everything going on in your life:

- What music are you listening to?
- What TV shows are you watching?
- What video games are you playing?
- Who are you hanging out with?
- What is it that you're putting in your body?
- What are you doing with your free time?

You're a very sensitive being, Indigo. Every aspect of what you do with your time affects your energy. It's not as if we as Indigos have any disabilities, but we're not like "normal" people. We can't just put junk in our body. We can't just turn on the TV and watch any old thing. We can't just listen to whatever angry, lower-energy music we want to.

If you are an Indigo who feels that you are struggling with keeping your energy high, one of the things you should definitely look into is who it is you are spending time around, and what is it you are doing with that time. What sort of energy is being perpetuated?

Are you focusing too much on the politics of the world, on talking about the problems and devoting countless hours to brooding about what you don't like in the world, and just inhabiting that energy? Or are you a person who knows that there should be changes in this world and knows that you'll make whatever changes you can along your path, but in the meantime you go easy on yourself and allow yourself to just be relaxed about the world around you, trusting that the change is happening *with* you?

We have to realize that because we have such heightened sensitivity, everything that would affect a regular person by one degree will affect us by 100 degrees. You just have to accept the fact that your gifts do come at a small price—a sense of normalcy—and you have a responsibility to really take care of yourself.

I compare it to a regular-manufacturer automobile, like any old Toyota or Ford driving down the street, versus a Lamborghini.

A Lamborghini is a very high-performance vehicle. While it's capable of doing the same things that any of the more mass-production, mainstream-type vehicles can do, it requires specialized service. It requires specialized parts and fluids in order for its finely tuned engine and mechanics to function correctly.

Yes, it's kind of a funny analogy, but since the Indigos came here with such powerful warrior energy, they are more like the exotic sports cars of the human world. If you try to put regular, rock-bottom gasoline in one of these super-expensive sports cars, you're going to have a lot of problems.

Indigos, when we feed ourselves this lower energy—taking part in fear-based conversations, allowing negative thoughts to run through our heads, putting all this junk in our bodies—then at some point we have to take responsibility for that. We shouldn't wonder why we can't find happiness, why our morale is so low, or why it's so easy for us to feel depressed or upset.

As Indigos, we need to take pride in ourselves and take care of our well-being. Think of yourself as that exotic sports car. Would you put junk oil and junk fuel inside a highly tuned sports car? Wouldn't you only put in the best? (No jokes about gas prices or oil or anything right here. It's only a metaphor, but it's an applicable one.)

Because Indigos come here with such a high purpose, they are gifted with heightened intuition, sensitivity, and awareness of their surroundings. In order for these gifts to *act* as gifts, the energy Indigos expose themselves to has to in every way be of the highest caliber.

I'll be honest with you: It was hard for me to accept that. I wanted to just eat at McDonald's. I wanted to just listen to whatever music I felt like, watch bad stories on the news, tune in to scary shows. I wanted to be normal.

I wanted to be like everyone else, and I tried that. But as I hear time and time again in testimony from other Indigos, parents, and caretakers, we just don't have that level of flexibility. We have to live on a higher plane and vibration.

We *have* to incorporate clean living and exercise. We have to meditate in some way. We have to use positive affirmations. We have to deploy discipline to correct any of our negative thoughts, to allow ourselves to believe that life can be better than the way it is right now.

How can Indigos deal with others' perceptions?

As an Indigo, when you're out and about in your daily life, it's really important to be aware of how natural it is for you to constantly compare yourself to others and also constantly be conscious of what you think others are thinking about you. Indigos have such busy minds that it's very easy for us to not only be occupied with whatever it is that we're doing, whatever our immediate goals are, but also be so aware of the energy around us.

When I was concerned with what people thought about me, when I would walk around in the world and my general sense of incompatibility with society would heighten my sensitivity to people's reactions to my presence, one of the things that helped me the most was when I was told that generally people spend more time thinking the same thing in their own heads. When you make eye contact with a stranger, there's a really good chance that, instead of judging you, they're themselves wondering if you're judging them, if you're thinking about *them*.

What I'm getting at here is that it's very important to not overly focus on the way we think the world is judging us, the way we think the world is looking at us—to really learn to be relaxed and detached from the way in which people might react to our energy and just be okay with ourselves.

How can Indigos avoid social isolation?

A lot of Indigos talk to me about how they feel antisocial. They feel agoraphobic. This is something that comes up that I really wanted to take the time to talk about because it's a very common scenario for Indigos to shut down and almost reject society and begin to spend a lot of time isolated.

This can be such a damaging way of life for Indigos on many levels that we should explore some positive alternatives to being antisocial. As I've previously discussed, being a parent or a caretaker of Indigos means that there are extra sets of responsibilities in helping to empower them and nurture their energy to be as effective and positive as possible.

As an Indigo yourself, you also have an extra and heightened responsibility to honor your own energy because it can feel so natural for Indigos to reject society as a whole, to reject the idea of socializing, to reject the idea of having friends and having social obligations.

You may not consider yourself lonely due to your rejection of society; but believe it or not, the isolation has a damaging effect on your soul and actually detracts from your ability to access and express the higher energy your soul craves and desires.

Even though I say I try to stay away from blanket prescriptions for helping Indigos find more joy in life and find a better sense of belonging, one thing I often share, which all Indigos should at least consider, is that socializing, as much as it may not have any appeal to you, can actually do you a lot of good.

I don't mean just going out and making friends for the sake of sitting around a table and talking about things that don't interest you. I'm talking about finding something that *does* interest you. Start there, maybe taking a painting class or woodworking class, maybe learning a musical instrument or learning how to sing, dance, or play some kind of sport.

I can guarantee that if you dig deep enough and you think about this long enough, there's some interest that you have that could be translated into a social situation. In a society, in a world with seven billion people in it, there's a better chance than not that you can find a like-minded group of people also interested in the same things.

I want to suggest that Indigos put some effort into forcing themselves to at least be a little social, because what happens when we isolate ourselves, even though we feel the comfort of not being susceptible to all of the energy that we pick up on, everything that causes us to be so sensitive when we're out in society, it's actually shutting down our energy.

We begin this shutdown. Our light, our soul, begins to dim as a result.

What happens is a lot of Indigos turn to the Internet and social networking as a form of replacing traditional social behavior. While this can have a pacifying effect, giving us the impression that we're socializing with people, especially on sites like Facebook, Twitter, and Reddit, it's furthering our sense of detachment from society.

Isolating ourselves from the people we think are causing us to feel depressed and upset can have the opposite effect from the desired one. It can backfire on us. It can lead to *more* depression.

As Indigos, believe it or not, we are extremely social beings. Now, follow along with me: The reason that we isolate ourselves, the reason that we feel antisocial is not because we don't like people; it's because we're disappointed in what we see. We're disappointed in the way that people treat each other.

We have higher expectations for the world around us than the average person. You may or may not be aware of that, but if you think about the reasons why you feel anti-social, I almost guarantee you that it is based in some level of disappointment, some level of hurt, because your soul purpose aims so high.

It's to create a world that has such a high vibration that we, again, reject the social norm, the shallowness, and the vanity of modern-day society to the point where we isolate ourselves from it.

What is the alternative to isolation?

It's important that Indigos begin to seek out other Indigos, not only by doing things, but also by taking additional actions, like creating a forum where Indigos can talk to each other, where they can relate with each other, so that they can can interact human to human. Forming outside, real-life social networks, instead of staying on the Internet, is what is going to keep the energy and the spirit of our souls alive.

You know deep down within you that if you could find a group of like-minded people, people with similar interests, with similar frustrations and tolerances, you would jump at every chance to socialize with those people.

I hate to break it to you. As antisocial as you think you are, you're actually not antisocial. You're quite social. You're just disappointed. You're hiding from a world that you don't agree with.

I invite you to get in touch with the fact that your soul is actually yearning for social interaction—and not by poking someone on Facebook or sending a tweet, but by real, tangible human interaction.

If you can find at least one interest that would give you a reason to actually leave the threshold of your house on a regular basis and socialize with people, you'll eventually find that it serves to increase your sense of well-being, confidence, and general pleasure in being alive by leaps and bounds.

Is the world hopeless?

If you, as an Indigo, are feeling that the world is hopeless, that there's no place for you in it, the "good" news—aside from the fact that you're definitely not alone—is that you're not completely *wrong*.

There *is* no place for any higher-vibrational being in a world that is so addicted to lower energy. But your job is to change that—just by being who you are, just by asking the questions you ask, just by refusing to take things at face value, by using your mind before you let yourself believe something.

You're making a difference. You're making a magnificent difference through change that this world has needed for thousands of years. When people look back at this time in history 200 years from now, they'll see just how brave so many souls were to go against the grain when society wanted nothing more than for them to put their heads down and not make a scene, not be noticed, not do anything that wasn't "normal."

These brave souls are standing up and saying, "Just because things aren't horrible doesn't mean they're perfect." We've been force-fed that pacifying thought process for too long. *Things could always be worse*, they say. Of course things could be worse, but does that mean that they couldn't be better?

Until all of humanity has access to the fulfillment of life, to the fulfillment of purpose, there's going to be more and more work to be done.

Indigos, I'd like to give you this to think about. I don't know how many generations it's going to take for the Indigo mission, for the Indigo goals, to actually take hold on this planet. It may happen in our lifetime. It may happen in our children's lifetime. I don't know.

We've already seen a lot of major changes, so I'm very optimistic that we're going to continue to see more—and the world is full of surprises. Considering that we, as Indigos, have such a monumental task, it's not outside the realm of logic to also consider that karmically we'll be assigned to come back again and again as Indigos with the same task until it is complete.

Yes, you can think of that as an overwhelming, daunting sense of obligation, but you can also think about it in a sense that you're here right now. You've already gone through birth, infancy. You were a toddler. You learned how to talk. You learned how to walk. Ideally, you got potty-trained. (That was my one joke for the book.)

You're already here. You've already accomplished so much, so why not let this lifetime be the absolute most effective that it can be? Why not make the biggest difference possible? Why not ruffle the most feathers you can?

Are Indigos at odds with society?

Obviously, there's an aspect of society that we have to go along with. If we constantly keep ourselves at the periphery of the world, how are we going to get deep enough inside to make the necessary changes? We're not. Get off the sidelines and play the game. Just play along. It's actually fun.

You start to realize that that's what everybody else is doing. You'll actually start to gain more respect for other humans. From the outside, it looks like they take this world so seriously, but when you actually get inside and dig around, you realize that there's almost no one alive right now who would not agree on some level that major changes could be made, that there could be more balance, that things could be structured in a way that actually takes care of the individual more.

All these idealistic notions you hear people talk about are what the Indigos are here to bring into being, because everybody wants it. Everybody's on your side, Indigo. You might feel that behaviorally or socially you're on the fringes, but when it comes down to your mission, you've got the entire world behind you.

When enough Indigos stand up and begin to make changes, as we're already seeing in the world today, everybody will stand up behind them. You'll go from feeling like a martyr to feeling like a hero, because you're making a tangible difference in a world that needs it.

What can Indigos do to adapt socially?

Don't feel triggered by previous models, by the previous evolution of humans who could maintain and sustain a life of lower ego energy, because they are overwhelmingly becoming the minority. They are overwhelmingly the people who are perpetuating an energy that is no longer fit for this world, that's no longer fit for the awakening and the spiritual evolution that's happening on this planet. Whether you are spiritual or not, you are going to see the changes this spiritual awakening is making and is going to continue to make in large strides.

Indigo, we need to learn to channel our anger in constructive ways. We need to learn to control our reactions to the aspects of this world that trigger us because, unfortunately, they are not going to go away right away.

That's just a codified dynamic in this world, something that most people don't like yet are able to ignore; and sometimes by ignoring behavior, you condone it. You in a subtle way give people permission to keep acting that way. Well, Indigo, you know that if you don't feel right about someone, and that's a consistent feeling, your guidance is telling you to make different choices.

As an Indigo myself, I've struggled with this. I've struggled with finding a group of people I felt resonated with *truth*: who were true to themselves, who were true to each other, who were honest, good people. It took a little while, but now my life is full of amazing people who are such a gift to me. But I never would have found them if I allowed myself to believe that I wouldn't, if I never actually put energy specifically into attracting them.

Even though the transition from hanging out with lower-energy people to spending time with higher-energy people wasn't the easiest, knowing that I have some of the most synchronistic, reciprocal friendships a human could ask for is one of the best rewards of my life.

It's one of the things that I am most grateful for. Indigo, don't be afraid to be picky, but don't go into anger. Don't blame society; don't start withdrawing just because aspects of society trigger your Indigo alarm. It's very important that you remember this.

Don't run away. Society needs you. As I am saying over and over again, there is a place for you in it. There are people you will resonate with. It *is* possible to have peace with family, if you can just breathe. It *is* possible to have peace in the workplace, if you can just tell yourself, *This is what I am here to change. It may be unpleasant, but this is what I am here to change.*

How can Indigos deal with conflict constructively?

When faced with disagreements, conflict, and arguments in more permanent settings such as the workplace, school, and at home, Indigos sometimes react to things as if they were always going to be that way.

That just has a lot to do with the intensity of the emotions that the Indigos feel—that sometimes in the heat of a moment, it's difficult for an Indigo to rationalize the situation, and they will react harsher because they feel trapped. They feel that this is the way things always will be, and because it feels so daunting and permanent, it makes things feel so much more intense for the Indigo.

As an Indigo, when you are in these scenarios, if you are fighting with family or if you are having a workplace conflict or some teacher or another student in school is causing you problems, it's really important to, number one, realize how temporary the situation is.

It may feel permanent. You might be thinking, *Well, I am only 12 years old, so that means at best I've got 6 more years to deal with this.* But anything and everything can change in an instant. *Nothing* is permanent.

Even though it may seem as if the dynamics that are causing you this level of grief or causing you to be so upset will never change, I can guarantee you that they will. I can guarantee you that whatever it is that you are going through in the workplace, in the school or family scenario, is so temporary that there will come a day when you won't even remember it.

If you're raised in a dysfunctional family, ultimately it's a temporary part of your life. You will spend more time in your life *not* living with your family than you will living with them. While acting out feels like a natural reaction to this unhealthy situation, you've got to consider the consequences for your future. Find peace in knowing that one day this situation will be over, and you will have the choice of being independent and choosing who you live with.

It's really important for you to stay conscious of that, because we need to put everything into a literal and accurate perspective. Because we feel things so intensely, we need to occasionally step aside energetically from a situation and remind ourselves that this is temporary. This is one of the most freeing mind-sets that an Indigo can allow themselves to be in. As a child, it's not your job to fix things or change people. Don't absorb the pressure your guardians are imposing upon you. Don't forget to be a kid, and go play and enjoy yourself.

Now, that's one step that can really help with the intensity in the way that we react to a situation. Since the intensity of our reaction tends to govern the intensity of the response to our actions, the calmer we can be, generally the calmer things will remain.

Do Indigos have special powers of manifestation?

I can guarantee that you know how you want your life to feel, that you want balance, you want truth, you want clarity, you want synchronicity. I know exactly what it is that you feel that you want for your life. You can use just those feelings to attract exactly that into your life. I promise you, Indigo, that you can maintain the discipline to shift your thoughts to be positive, to be optimistic, and refuse to think about anything negative—it's a waste of your time. Know that. Tell yourself that: *That which does not serve me, that which does not resonate with me, is a waste of my time. As an Indigo, I refuse to use any of my precious energy focusing on any of the negative aspects of my life.*

When we can turn our thought process around and start thinking about possibilities and positivity, even if there doesn't seem to be hope, but if we can just let ourselves believe that there is—if we can consistently maintain this in our mind-set, we are going to manifest changes. You will manifest healthier, more harmonious situations in your family and at school.

You can manifest a healthier workplace. You can manifest living exactly where you want. You can manifest anything you want. There are no limitations, aside from whatever fear you have about your ability to manifest. But, Indigo, I am here to tell you right now that you are gifted in the sense of manifestation. You should learn to use this, to not only benefit your own life, but also to benefit every scenario where you feel that wrong is being done.

How does manifestation actually work?

You don't have to be spiritual. You don't have to believe in angels. The law of attraction is actually a universal law, and it really doesn't have a lot to do with anything other than the way the universe works. Everything in the universe is about attraction. That's how matter exists. That's how atoms stick together. Our power as Indigos, our power as humans, is that we can work with and control attraction through the energy of our thoughts.

Think about it. Everything in the universe is made of protons, neutrons, and electrons, everything. *You* are made of protons, neutrons, and electrons. Your thoughts are made of these same atoms.

Why should we allow ourselves to believe that there is any difference between anything that we could ever want in life and our thoughts? On a molecular level there *is* no difference. Believe that since your thoughts are made of the same material that everything else is, your thoughts can attract whatever it is that you want.

Your thoughts can attract love; your thoughts can attract peace, harmony, balance, affluence, if you so desire. Whatever you want, you just have to believe it—you just have to shift your mind-set away from a natural anger and frustration that might seem so easy to fall into and force yourself to think positively. Now, this is another one of those exercises that literally costs you nothing.

You've got nothing to lose by trying this. But, Indigo, if you can put the same intensity you've used to fight the world around you into thinking about what you would change, about how you would improve your own life and the lives of those you care about, and you put that energy out there, you will be absolutely amazed to watch these changes come to fruition.

There is no point in being skeptical about this, because if you think about the mainstream mind-set that would be skeptical of the law of attraction, you are living in the world that that mainstream thought created. The best that mainstream thought can do is the world that you see around you. It's the world where people bomb each other, where people shoot each other.

It's the world that we want to change. It's the world that we need to bring peace to. If there was any credibility to mainstream thought, if mainstream thought was the pinnacle of human ideals, we'd be living in a much better world right now. It's time for new thought; it's time for us literally as humans to stop the insanity. The definition of insanity is doing the same thing over and over again and expecting different results.

One of my favorite sayings I've ever heard is: *To get something that you've never had, you've got to do something that you've never done.*

What we as humans—not just Indigos, as *humans*—need to do is shift our mind-set and allow ourselves to believe in a better world, to believe in peace, to believe that there can be more unity, more connection. Until we do so, we can't feel like victims, we can't blame anyone but ourselves, because when it comes down to it, who is out there writing the rules besides us? No one.

Indigo, we are here to lead the charge. When you give yourself permission to experience the magnificent change that you are capable of bringing in with your thoughts, with your intentions, with your desires, you are going to start to realize just how powerful you are, and you are going to start using that power for good.

What is Indigo Power?

A sense of purpose is probably one of the most healing and calming aspects of life that an Indigo can get in touch with. Hopefully, just hearing about the amazing phenomenon of the influx of Indigo energy into this world can help you realize that you are part of something amazing.

Whether you realize it or not, everything about you is a gift to this world. The Indigo energy is what this planet has been waiting for. Finally we have a group of souls, a group of people, who are going to integrate themselves into society but refuse to just take it at face value.

These souls are going to dig through the etheric archives of our way of life and make sure that every policy, every rule, every standard, every practice, every moral, every value that is sometimes blindly perpetuated by everyday society is forensically examined and only allowed to stay in place if it isn't archaic and serves our modern-day desires.

It is through this change that the lightworkers of this world are going to be able to replace the old rules with new, lighter, more applicable ways of being so that we can finally collectively create the world that we all know we are meant to exist in—a world of peace, a world of connection, a world of love, and a world of harmony.

It is possible, and the catalyst for the necessary change is here on this planet. Our job now is just to be human, just to go through our lives aware of the power of higher energy, of our power to attract whatever exists in our thoughts.

As this knowledge continues to spread, and as more and more people wake up to the truth of our existence—that we *have* purpose—and begin to pursue harmony and find fulfillment in their lives, we will experience magnificent changes on this planet that are going to bring a sustainable level of world peace.

Thank you so much for reading. Thank you so much for being a part of the Indigo awareness movement. Many blessings to you.

AN INDIGO AFTERWORD

by Charles

Being Indigo, I am sometimes placed in some very interesting situations—and as most Indigos know, our feelings about a given situation are often difficult, if not impossible, to hide. I find myself extremely conflicted on a regular basis. My mission and purpose right now are to travel and teach about angels—I have been exposed to this most of my life. It is my passion, and I love what I do; however, I do not always love what I see.

Now, before I elaborate, let me make it clear that I know that love and light is *the* way to be; it is the future of humanity. But as an Indigo, I also know that we will never get there if we sit complacently waiting for it to dawn.

I have had the honor of working with some amazing people around the world in my short time as a teacher. My heart has opened up so many times to the passion, power, and loving nature of *so* many of my students. And in my classes I am always adamant, and even repetitive, about telling everyone that the world needs you, and if you feel guided to be a lightworker, consider yourself one now.

According to follow-up e-mails and conversations, people find that for the most part the guidance to make this major life change comes easily when they just let go and let the angels lead them there.

But notable numbers of people find themselves road-blocked by an unfortunate side effect of anything popular in this world: corporate greed.

This Afterword is not intended to portray companies in a bad light; it is meant to empower *you* as an Indigo, as a lightworker.

We all need to know that if we are guided to share a message, there is a Divine reason for it. If you are feeling called to teach, write, or speak, it is because you have answers the world needs. Your audience will find you. They are asking the questions right now, and if you are not answering them, the link is broken. With the power of the Web and social media, anyone can instantly have worldwide exposure from their living room. So start sharing, start writing, start planning your classes, and the universe will open doors to show you your place.

Today I want to challenge you. I want you to step outside your comfort zone and say a quick prayer: *"How can I help the world?"*

Sit patiently and wait for the answer. Write down what you get, and start doing it. Post it on social media, put it on your blog, talk about it in your videos—any avenue, as long as you express your truth publicly!

The angels are always there to guide us along our journey, but they are not here to live life for us. If we want to go the distance, we must start taking steps, even blind ones, in that direction. The angels' guidance will come to us to shed light on our path and remind us that we are here for a reason. As my mother says, "You are all needed *now*."

ENDNOTES

Lesson 1

1. D. Virtue. *The Care and Feeding of Indigo Children.* Carlsbad, CA: Hay House, Inc., 2001.

Lesson 3

1. D. Virtue. *Don't Let Anything Dull Your Sparkle.* Carlsbad, CA: Hay House, Inc., 2015.

Lesson 4

1. J. Dungan, et al. "The Psychology of Whistleblowing." *Current Opinion in Psychology*, 2015, 6: 129–133.

2. "Hawaii's Largest Commercial Beekeeper Fires Worker for Launching Crowdfunding Campaign to Save Bees." *The Sleuth Journal*, June 1, 2016. Retrieved from: www.thesleuthjournal.com/ hawaiis-largest-commercial-beekeeper-fires-worker-for-launching -crowdfunding-campaign-to-save-bees.

Lesson 6

1. "How Many Teens and Other Youth Are Vegetarian and Vegan? The Vegetarian Resource Group Asks in a 2014 National Poll." *The Vegetarian Research Group Blog*, May 30, 2014. Retrieved from: www.vrg.org/blog/2014/05/30/how-many-teens-and-other-youth -are-vegetarian-and-vegan-the-vegetarian-resource-group-asks-in-a -2014-national-poll.

ABOUT THE AUTHORS

Doreen Virtue holds B.A., M.A., and Ph.D. degrees in counseling psychology and is a lifelong clairvoyant and Christian mystic. A former psychotherapist, Doreen now gives online workshops on topics related to her books and oracle cards. She's the author of *The Courage to Be Creative, Don't Let Anything Dull Your Sparkle, Assertiveness for Earth Angels, The Miracles of Archangel Michael,* and *Archangel Oracle Cards,* among many other works. She has appeared on *Oprah,* CNN, the BBC, *The View,* and *Good Morning America* and has been featured in newspapers and magazines worldwide.

For information on Doreen's work, please visit her at AngelTherapy.com or Facebook.com/DoreenVirtue444. To enroll in Doreen's video courses, please visit www.Hay HouseU.com and www.EarthAngel.com.

ANGEL THERAPY®

Charles Virtue is the eldest son of Doreen Virtue and the author of the forthcoming book *Manifesting with the Angels.* He is also the co-author of *Signs from Above* and *Indigo Angel Oracle Cards,* the creator of *Manifesting with Archangel Nathaniel* audio class, and the co-teacher of online video courses about Indigos and discovering your life purpose for HayHouseU. Since 2007, Charles has lectured about angels, life purpose, healing, manifestation, teacher training, and Indigos in over 20 countries and has appeared on television and radio programs and in newspapers and magazines internationally. More is available on his website: www.CharlesVirtue.com.

Hay House Titles of Related Interest

YOU CAN HEAL YOUR LIFE, the movie,
starring Louise Hay & Friends
(available as a 1-DVD program and an expanded 2-DVD set)
Watch the trailer at: www.LouiseHayMovie.com

THE SHIFT, the movie, starring Dr. Wayne W. Dyer
(available as a 1-DVD program and an expanded 2-DVD set)
Watch the trailer at: www.DyerMovie.com

*AWAKENED BY AUTISM: Embracing Autism, Self,
and Hope for a New World,* by Andrea Libutti, M.D.

*BEATING BIPOLAR: How One Therapist Tackled His Illness . . .
and How What He Learned Could Help You!,* by Blake LeVine

*HEAL YOUR CHILD FROM THE INSIDE OUT:
The 5-Element Way to Nurturing Healthy, Happy Kids,*
by Robin Ray Green, L.Ac., MTCM

THE INDIGO CHILDREN: The New Kids Have Arrived and
*THE INDIGO CHILDREN TEN YEARS LATER:
What's Happening with the Indigo Teenagers!,*
by Lee Carroll and Jan Tober

THE LAST DROPOUT: Stop the Epidemic!, by Bill Milliken

LET IT OUT: A Journey Through Journaling, by Katie Dalebout

*MEMORIES OF HEAVEN: Children's Astounding
Recollections of the Time Before They Came to Earth,*
by Dr. Wayne W. Dyer and Dee Garnes

THROUGH INDIGO'S EYES and
BECOMING INDIGO,
by Tara Taylor and Lorna Schultz Nicholson

All of the above are available at your local bookstore,
or may be ordered by contacting Hay House (see next page).

We hope you enjoyed this Hay House book. If you'd like to receive our online catalog featuring additional information on Hay House books and products, or if you'd like to find out more about the Hay Foundation, please contact:

Hay House, Inc., P.O. Box 5100, Carlsbad, CA 92018-5100
(760) 431-7695 or (800) 654-5126
(760) 431-6948 (fax) or (800) 650-5115 (fax)
www.hayhouse.com® • www.hayfoundation.org

Published and distributed in Australia by:
Hay House Australia Pty. Ltd., 18/36 Ralph St., Alexandria NSW 2015
Phone: 612-9669-4299 • *Fax:* 612-9669-4144 • www.hayhouse.com.au

Published and distributed in the United Kingdom by:
Hay House UK, Ltd., Astley House, 33 Notting Hill Gate, London W11 3JQ
Phone: 44-20-3675-2450 • *Fax:* 44-20-3675-2451 • www.hayhouse.co.uk

Published and distributed in the Republic of South Africa by:
Hay House SA (Pty), Ltd., P.O. Box 990, Witkoppen 2068
info@hayhouse.co.za • www.hayhouse.co.za

Published in India by: Hay House Publishers India,
Muskaan Complex, Plot No. 3, B-2, Vasant Kunj, New Delhi 110 070
Phone: 91-11-4176-1620 • *Fax:* 91-11-4176-1630 • www.hayhouse.co.in

Distributed in Canada by:
Raincoast Books, 2440 Viking Way, Richmond, B.C. V6V 1N2
Phone: 1-800-663-5714 • *Fax:* 1-800-565-3770 • www.raincoast.com

Take Your Soul on a Vacation

Visit www.HealYourLife.com® to regroup, recharge,
and reconnect with your own magnificence.
Featuring blogs, mind-body-spirit news,
and life-changing wisdom from Louise Hay and friends.

Visit www.HealYourLife.com today!